SMALL ACTIONS, BIG RESULTS

Ashdin Doctor is the Habit Coach™. He believes awesome lives start with awesome habits. He is the author of three bestselling titles—*Change Your Habits, Change Your Life, The Book of Good Habits for Kids* and *One Habit A Day*.

He also hosts the award-winning podcast, *The Habit Coach*, which has over 1,200 episodes. It's ranked amongst the top self-development podcasts in India and covers a wide variety of topics all designed to help the listener evolve through their daily habits.

Ashdin works with people from all across the world, helping them with their habits, spreading his message through keynote speeches, workshops and group coachings. Apart from habit coaching, he is a director at Ormax Consultants Pvt. Ltd, Ormax Media Pvt. Ltd and Ormax Evolve Pvt. Ltd. He is also a trustee at the Light of Life Trust, an NGO dedicated to the care of underprivileged children around the world, and will be donating a percentage of the proceeds from this book to the NGO to promote literacy.

BASED ON THE POPULAR IVM PODCAST, THE HABIT COACH™

ASHDIN DOCTOR

SMALL ACTIONS, BIG RESULTS

31 Habits for a Supercharged Life

Published by Westland Books, a division of Nasadiya Technologies Private Limited, in 2024

No. 269/2B, First Floor, 'Irai Arul', Vimalraj Street, Nethaji Nagar, Alapakkam Main Road, Maduravoyal, Chennai 600095

Westland and the Westland logo are the trademarks of Nasadiya Technologies Private Limited, or its affiliates.

ISBN: 9789360459543

10 9 8 7 6 5 4 3 2 1

Typeset by Jojy Philip, New Delhi

Printed at Thomson Press (India) Ltd

Contents

Introduction

In a world filled with distractions, the ability to focus becomes the new secret to success. This workbook is filled with habits that will help you focus your attention on getting things done. It will help you take those small steps that can have the biggest impact on your life. Be it the ability to focus at work or at home with your family.

After the incredible success of my first workbook, *One Habit A Day,* which focused on habits to make you mentally strong and resilient, I decided to write a workbook focused on making your life easier. In this book, I've brought together small habits that, if incorporated in your life, can make a huge difference and lead to attaining the biggest results.

I recommend you read it and work on the exercises given at the end of each chapter. As a Habit Coach™, I am all about putting knowledge into action. Learning something and not using it is a waste. My podcast *The Habit Coach* is also based on the same principle. I believe that is the reason it was awarded the Best Motivational and Self-Help Podcast.

If you don't enjoy reading too much, I recommend you read just one chapter every day. Find a place at home or at work where you can sit undisturbed for 15 minutes and read a chapter. I believe you'll find them engaging and easy to implement.

I can't wait for you to begin reading and incorporating the ideas in this book into your life. It's my hope that it will lead to a new, productive and supercharged you!

Your Habit Coach,
Ashdin Doctor

Attention!

Here's a fun fact to do with military marching: marching was introduced so soldiers would not get lost. Back in the day, foot soldiers were the main fighting force of an army. In order to go to battle, soldiers had to cover large distances on foot. They had to set up camps, cross rivers and mountain passes, deal with all sorts of weather—you get the drift.

Very often, on the way to battle, an army's fighting force would begin to dwindle. Say 2,000 men would start off for the battle but only 1,800 of them would arrive. Two hundred men would have been lost along the way. Lost not to death, but just lost. They might have taken the wrong path or stayed at one camp too long, not arriving at the battlefield on time.

This led to the invention of marching, where the whole fighting force was broken up into smaller groups that stayed and walked together. Soon the walking tempo was drilled into the soldiers so that the commanders had an accurate understanding of the speed at which the whole force was moving.

Marching practice was part of my school life. I hated it, taking part in it only so I could bunk a few classes. I would wonder what was the point of us learning how to walk in this funny manner. I would often lose my timing with the rest of the group. Left, left, left, right, left. Ah, the thought of it brings back memories of the dusty grounds we practiced in.

One of the commands rings in my ears till this day: Attention! As a child, it meant nothing to me. But as an adult wanting to build good habits for myself, it is something that I focus on a lot. Back then 'attention' was just a word but now I have realised that it is a superpower. Attention defines the quality of our lives. Our lives take the direction in which we employ our attention.

If you think about it, you'll find that the biggest businesses of our time are all attention-based businesses. Instagram, news channels, Twitter, YouTube, Netflix, casinos, online shopping, porn. Each worth billions and trillions of dollars. Each using only one real currency—your attention.

Different people pay attention to different things in their lives. Someone may be devoting all their attention towards finding the best ways to outsmart people or even to con them, another may be looking for ways in which they can make a quick buck. Some people are trying to get more than they deserve. Notice if your mind is like this. If it's always trying to do more. If that is the case, then it's a mind that can never be calm because it is never satisfied. It is a mind that makes a living hell for itself and for people around.

Then there are the people who don't, or aren't able to, give any direction to their attention. These blabbermouths just keep talking without thinking. They speak a lot, but in the end, have said nothing. They are very distracted and disoriented. They forget where they've put things and they are clumsy. They are not attentive towards their body or towards the world around them. A person like that is never at ease because they don't feel like their life is going anywhere. This is because their attention is not going anywhere.

The third are the rigid fanatics. Their attention is on one thing and one thing only. If you talk to them about something else, they will ignore you and totally dismiss you. And this does not have to be about religion. We have people who are fanatic about their work. We have exercise fanatics who only focus on exercising and protein shakes all day and night. We have all kinds of fanatics. You would know such people who are living lives that are just one shade. No change, no character. Utterly boring.

The fourth are the worriers. They only think about the problems. They are constantly fearful—of the future, the past, of their life, of their dog, cat, family, of anything and everything. If there is nothing to worry about, they will worry about that as well. These kinds of people destroy perfect relationships because they don't believe that it can be this good. But more importantly because they are looking for the problem in everything. How can a worrier be peaceful and calm? Their attention is on the negative and they cannot see the positive in anything.

Now I want you to think about these four. Do you know people who fall into these categories? Which category do you fall into? You could even be a mix of two or more categories. There will, however, be one dominant part. That is where your attention resides.

As your habit coach, I want you to learn about attention and be aware of where you spend your attention. Think of attention as money. If you wake up and have attention worth a thousand dollars, where do you end up spending it throughout the day? Is it spent on distractions like porn and TV? Is it spent on cunning? Is it spent on your loved ones, worrying and obsessing about them?

Learning where your attention resides and altering it, if needed, can change the course of your life.

So your super simple habit is to identify where you spend your attention each and every day. Then I want you to identify three worthy goals or tasks that deserve your attention. I want you to move your attention to these goals every day.

I'll leave you with a small tip. Every time you catch your attention being spent on useless things, I want you to shift your focus and shout: Attention!

Exercise

What kind of worrier are you? Which of the four types resonated the most with you?

____

____

____

Where do you see your attention slipping away to on most days? Which activity distracts your attention from the things that will make your life awesome?

____

____

____

What is the one thing that needs your full attention? Think about that one thing that will completely transform your life, if you were to give it your attention.

____

____

____

Be Like Water

Here's a fun fact: the most dangerous animal in the Grand Canyon is the rock squirrel. That's right—a small furry little squirrel!

While the canyon is home to much larger animals, like the bighorn sheep, it is this pesky little bugger that causes the most trouble. Every year many tourists are attacked and bitten by these squirrels. The squirrels want food that the tourists carry.

To make things worse, the tourists feed these squirrels and get attacked in the process. Talk about biting the hand that feeds you!

When I had visited Yosemite National Park, I saw warning signs that read 'Do not feed the bears.' Bears being dangerous I can understand. But squirrels?

What I find really fascinating about the Grand Canyon is how it was made. This beautiful national park has an 'otherworldly' feel to it. Visitors find themselves in awe of its size. Once there, you can feel how you are a tiny speck in this universe.

The Grand Canyon was carved out over 6 million years ago by mainly one thing—the Colorado River. Over hundreds of years, the river slowly ate away at the rocks, wearing them down to form the canyons we see today.

There are two amazing properties of water that fascinate me. The first is that water is persistent. It doesn't stop doing what it has to do. Most of the time that is finding a way to go from a higher place to a lower place. It's close to impossible to stop it. You have to build huge monstrous dams. And even then, sometimes it will break through.

It is persistent.

The second principle of water is that it takes the path of least resistance. It chooses the easiest way out. Water will continue to flow through the gaps and crevices and find the easiest way around an obstacle. See the way a river flows; it goes past and around big mountains and rocks.

Now compare that with how we live. Very often we get into the habit of finding the hardest thing that we can do. We choose to do the most difficult things possible. Why? Because we have the need to feel worthy. We want to prove to others and ourselves that we can do these difficult things.

We set ourselves impossible goals with impossible deadlines. We work ourselves to the bone. Go through burnout. Have heart attacks. And then form bad habits like binge eating and binge drinking to deal with these difficult goals we have set for ourselves.

Over the years we have trained ourselves to choose goals and objectives that are hard to accomplish. Hence, we have created a habit of thinking in this particular way. I know this is something that I was guilty of. Choosing the hardest possible goal and then choosing the hardest possible way to get at it. When you think about it, it is such a silly thing to do.

Think about all the things you are doing and the goals you are setting. As your habit coach, I want you to achieve all of them, and not have them affect your health.

So what I want you to do is ask yourself one question: What is the easiest way of achieving this goal? It is such a simple question but a powerful one. What is the easiest way this thing can be done?

What is the path of least resistance to get this done?

It is something that we can learn from the Colorado River. It chose the path of least resistance and yet was able to carve out the Grand Canyon.

So your super simple habit starts by asking yourself a question for anything that you do: What is the easiest way of doing this thing? Sometimes the answer you'll arrive at will be: don't do it at all. And that is fine too. You will notice this one question will free up time and energy for you.

There is so much we can learn from water. Water has been like a guru to me. I have learnt so much just by observing the way it is. As Bruce Lee said: 'Be water, my friend.'

Exercise

Write down a goal you have been struggling with. Now write down next to it, the easiest possible way of achieving it.

1. ______________________________

2. ______________________________

3. ______________________________

What prevents you from being consistent and persistent in the pursuit of things you want to achieve? How can you add consistency and persistence back into your life? Spend time thinking about this and write it down. Is it a mindset change? Or a scheduling change?

____

____

____

Becoming an Active Reader

Do you know which is the longest book in the world? It's a French book called *À la recherche du temps perdu*. The English translation was first published under the title *A Remembrance of Things Past* and later as *In Search of Lost Time*. Yes, I'm talking about the book by Marcel Proust.

This book is recognised by Guinness World Records as the longest book. Character count is used to determine the record holder, and this book has a staggering 1.6 million characters or letters.

Can you imagine reading a book that heavy and dense? I go completely mad when I try reading those tomes. This record-holder of a book would probably be something you start enthusiastically but can't finish reading. How would you even remember what happened at the start of the book!

Does this ever happen to you? You are reading and reading and suddenly you realise you have forgotten what transpired in the earlier pages. So you go back and re-read it.

Or how about this? You put the book down for twenty minutes, go and make yourself a cup of coffee, come back and start reading. After about three paragraphs you realise that you have already read this.

All this back and forth causes you to lose interest in reading. My grandfather famously used to complain about this. He was a successful entrepreneur but uneducated so he had a hard time reading.

Every time my grandmother would call him he had to put down the book and re-read the last chapter when he got back to it. So he would always say that that was why he had never finished a book in his life.

Does this happen to you as well?

The reason this takes place is that we are not focused while reading. Our attention wanders towards what to make for dinner or that task on your to-do list. Reading becomes a passive, background activity.

We need to make reading more active and focused. There are a number of things you can do for this.

You can underline the words you are reading with your fingers or a closed pen. The same way we were taught how to read in school. The finger under the line follows the words you are reading. This makes you more mindful of the text you are reading.

Another thing you can do is highlight interesting lines. Or make notes on the side of the book when you find something interesting. This way it reinforces an idea back into your mind.

Or at the end of a chapter you can stop and try to recall what happened and what were the important things mentioned.

All these things take effort and may appear time-consuming. But, over the course of a book, re-reading the same things over again because you forgot what was mentioned is far more time consuming.

The way to keep track of active reading is to create a rule for yourself. The rule is that you will never re-read a paragraph or a page or a chapter. Once read, you will move on.

It doesn't matter if you can remember it or not. Never go back and re-read. This might sound crazy but being strict with yourself for a few books will make it easier going ahead.

So your super simple habit to start reading faster is to become an active reader. Never re-read the page again—this is the rule you read by. Use a tool to make sure you are completely focused and in the moment, while you read.

If you do not have the habit of reading, you can start by just reading one page a day. Start the habit small and easy!

If you are like my grandfather and find it hard completing books, this habit is for you. Active reading is such a joy.

Exercise

Make a commitment and write it down. 'I will never re-read a page, I will focus when reading it the first time.'

What are the books you are currently reading and want to read in the future?

Becoming an Olympian in Your Daily Life

The year 2024 was the year of Olympics. So how about a fun fact to do with the Olympics? Did you know that the former Soviet Union was one of the most dominant forces in the Olympics? And this is critical because they refused to participate in the Olympics before 1952, calling it a game for the bourgeoisie.

What is amazing about their participation is that their athletes would regularly dominate and bring home gold medals. This is especially true in the 1960 Olympics where they brought home a record forty-three gold medals and a total of 103 medals.

In the previous edition of the Olympics, their tally of medals was less than half.

One of the keys to this insane jump in medals was attributed to a new style of training that the Soviet Union had perfected. This style of training was called Periodisation.

It is a concept that was established in the 1950s by Hans Selye. He was an endocrinologist and worked on a theory called

General Adaptation Syndrome (GAS). Selye observed three stages in animals once they were exposed to a stressor.

The first stage, called the Alarm stage, involved the initial shock of the stressor on the system. The Resistance stage, which was the second stage, involved the animal adapting to the stress. In the third stage, called the Exhaustion stage, repairs are inadequate and a decrease in system function is observed.

This is a very powerful concept, as it states that for change to take place, we need some kind of stressor on the system. And this kind of stress is called Eustress.

Now two Soviet sports scientists took this idea and adapted it to training their athletes. They would make them focus on one particular exercise or format of training for a three-month period. These three months would create a stress on the system, as the athletes would try to adapt to the shock of training.

The body would then begin to adapt and change to this new style of training. The athletes grew stronger and better at the sport they were training for because of this technique called periodisation.

Athletes around the world would follow a different style of training where they would consistently practice all aspects of the sport without a focused period. As a result, they were not growing as fast as the Soviet athletes.

We can learn from this technique and use periodisation in our lives as well—especially when it comes to our professional lives. In order to grow and become more productive, we have to learn to push ourselves. Periodisation is a great way to do this.

Instead of stretching your goals out for the entire year, break them into four periods. In the first three months of the year, focus on one skill or technique you are trying to master, or one project you are trying to complete. For example, the first period could be spent in trying to become a better public speaker. So, during the first three months, join classes, make presentations, learn voice modulation, NLP techniques and so on. Keep your entire focus on just this one goal.

The next period might be about learning to delegate work, so you hire the right people or you learn how to not be in control of everything and micromanage life.

In the next period you might want to learn how to write powerfully. So you spend three months practising precisely that.

The key here is focus. For each of these three-month periods, you do nothing else but focus on that one goal you've picked for yourself for that period. Put yourself out of your comfort zone, and allow for the stress to build up. And then you will adapt.

I wrote my second book in this way. For three months I only focused on writing and completing it. It was the first time I was writing for kids so I spent the first month learning how to build characters, craft stories, talk to kids, etc. The second and third months were spent writing.

So your super simple habit for Olympic-style growth starts by breaking your yearly growth into four periods. Focus on one activity in each period to become awesome at it. Let the stress build up. Keep the focus so you are not distracted by different things.

Soon you will be amazed at how far you have come and what progress you have made. Don't try doing many things at the same time—that is a recipe for disaster. Keep the focus and use the power of periodisation.

Exercise

What are you training for? Is there a skill you need to master at work? Is there a hobby you are trying to get better at? What is a big goal you are moving towards?

What are the skills you need to develop to be able to achieve that goal? For the next three months focus only on developing those skills. Make it a single point of focus.

Start planning your path with three months of intense focused training and work and then recovery.

Clearing the Obstacles on the Path to Productivity

Are you someone who declutters their space regularly? If not, let me tell you a fun (or maybe a not-so-fun) fact. About 77 per cent of the people who live in cluttered and dysfunctional homes have a likelihood of being obese and overweight.

One of the causes of clutter is hoarding. Did you know that about 1.4 million people in America alone have been diagnosed with hoarding as a clinical disorder? What's interesting about hoarding is that people don't hoard because they are greedy. They do so out of fear. This fear is a strange life or death fear. In fact, if their hoarding behaviour is threatened by someone throwing something away, the hoarder immediately responds with anger.

Now, while we may not be hoarders living with seven-foot high piles of newspapers or 3,000 garden gnomes, we all tend to create clutter in our lives. Physical clutter in our room, on our desks, in the bathrooms. Mental clutter of half-finished tasks or conversations had in the past. Clutter on our phones with apps that we have downloaded and not used. The important thing to learn is that clutter grows and grows and grows. As you live you pick up things along the way. If you do not learn to put them down afterwards you end up with your hands full of things you don't really need.

It's like walking into a supermarket. You didn't take a shopping cart because you only wanted to buy some chewing gum. Fifteen minutes later, your arms are full and you have a packet of bread dangling from your mouth. You're dropping some things on the floor as you walk around.

Clutter is a part of life. What's more, we never use 80 per cent of the things we keep. We wear only 20 per cent of the clothes we own!

There are so many studies that show the effect of clutter on the productivity of individuals. In one, a disorderly room increased the creativity of the participants while an orderly room increased critical reasoning skill.

In a 2013 study, people in orderly rooms chose an apple over a chocolate 67 per cent of the time. Whereas, those in a cluttered room chose chocolate.

Chances are we do not realise our environment is cluttered. This is because we see it every day. We see things that do not belong where they are but don't put them away. Sometimes we even end up buying the same thing twice simply because we couldn't find the one we had bought the first time.

We keep telling ourselves that the next time we clean the house we'll organise better. However, there is never a next time.

My room has always been disorganised. My mom often jokes with me that the only time my room looks tidy is when I have an important meeting there or if I'm hosting a party. Yes, that's the only time I tidy up my room. I used to be proud of my mess and of the fact that, despite the mess, I knew where everything was. No longer.

The good news is that there are many different approaches to clearing clutter that are gaining popularity. Minimalism is one such approach. It means you only have what you absolutely need. There are a few multimillionaires who don't have a house to their name but prefer staying in Airbnb's. This is a very urban monk approach to life. The popularity of people like Marie Kondo is exploding. Marie Kondo recommends only keeping those things that spark joy. You can watch her series on Netflix and several of her videos are available on YouTube too.

I believe in having simple tiny habits, that compound over time into a great change. So I don't recommend starting off by giving away your stuff and turning into a monk. Instead, start with a simple principle: have a place for everything in your home.

Whenever you leave a room always pick up something that was out of place and put it away in its correct spot. If you enter the bathroom five times a day, that's five things you have organised.

It's a very simple tool and a great habit to form.

So your super simple habit for dealing with clutter is to always leave a room with something in your hand that you are putting into place. Soon you'll see the clutter around you decreasing. And you may just wonder, where did everything go? The thing is, everything you need will still be there; it will just be in its right place.

Exercise

Clear five things from your environment. It can either be in your room, your office or even in the bag you are carrying. Make a list of the items you get rid of.

Never leave a room without picking up something to clear and putting it in place. Do it mindfully till it becomes a habit.

Does Your Goal Matter?

Did you know that India follows the five-year plan as a way to focus on economic growth? The first five-year plan was made way back in 1951. These plans are used to revitalise the country's economy and sometimes redirect its focus. Some of the biggest changes in the country arose from these five-year plans.

Interestingly, the 1966–69 period was called the plan holiday. No five-year plans were executed during this time because of the India–Pakistan war.

The beauty of a five-year plan is that it gives one clear focus; one thing to target. It also allows for consistency; even if there is a change in the party in power at the Centre, it doesn't affect the implementation of the five-year plan.

All other plans can then lead from this bigger, broader goal or they can feed into this goal.

If there wasn't a clear long-term objective like this, then every time a new person or party came into power they would change things around based on their own ideas and ideology. The focus would disappear.

When you run after the latest craze, it becomes a burning desire. Have you noticed something like this happening in your life as well? You can't stop thinking about it; you just have to have it.

We often do this with our goals too. We end up setting up goals keeping the way we are feeling on that particular day in mind. Or we set a goal as a knee-jerk reaction from reading a new book that inspires us. Or someone we trust influences us in a decision.

Instead of having a focused direction to our lives we are now running around helter-skelter. Trying to search for the next best thing. Or something that gives us immediate gratification.

The problem is that as humans we often overestimate our ability in the short term. We give ourselves big crazy short-term goals, like lose ten kilos in two weeks. And we completely underestimate what can be done in the long term. In fact most of us don't have a long-term goal.

Imagine if instead of thinking about losing ten kilos in two weeks we could think about reversing obesity and having a good blood report in five years.

Our short-term goals need to have a long-term perspective. In fact, most of what we do should have a long-term perspective.

This does not mean obsessing about the future and not living in the present. It just means knowing the direction you want your life to take.

This can be done by asking yourself a simple question every time you set a goal for yourself: will this matter in the next five years? If the answer is no, think of something else to focus on instead. Or think of another way of doing what you wanted so that it is meaningful after five years.

As your habit coach I want you to learn this simple perspective shift. Delay your gratification, you will get more of it in the long run. Focus is the key to this kind of long-term success.

So your super simple habit to plan your goals better starts by asking yourself one simple question every time you want to create a new goal for yourself: will this matter in the next five years?

Get into the habit of thinking long term. Ask how will this goal affect me. And you'll notice the impact of it in your life.

Exercise

Close your eyes and imagine what your life could look like five years from now. What do you want to achieve? What is the quality of your life? What are the goals you need to set for yourself to get to this amazing life in five years?

Look at your current goals and ask yourself if they will really matter in five years. Write down the goals that will have the biggest impact five years later.

Don't Be a Pro(crastinator)

Did you know that the Navi Mumbai International Airport is one of the most delayed mega projects in the world? It has been delayed by nearly thirty years!

The idea of this project was to create an international airport outside the main city of Mumbai. By moving it outside, the size of the airport could be much larger.

The project was initiated in 1997 and suffered from several delays on various counts—from delay in the acquisition of land to residents of adjoining areas not moving out, financial troubles and, to top it all, the COVID-19 pandemic. At the time of writing of this book, the airport is still a few months away from being operational.

In our lives too, we often face delays. A project that we are working on in the office may not meet its planned timelines. Or there may be a side business we've been wanting to start for the last seven years but haven't got around to yet.

My family wanted to move to a bigger house. So we sold our old house and moved in to a rented apartment. It was to be our temporary home till we found a house to buy. Can you guess how long we spent in that rented apartment before finally getting our own house? Twelve years. Yes, you read that correctly!

Most of us procrastinate. The idea that 'I will do it later' is so appealing to us that we waste time and opportunities. Our deadlines whiz past us before we realise where all that time went.

Now, there are two main reasons why we may procrastinate: either the task is too difficult to do, or it is too easy. You may think how does that make sense. Well, the fact is that if something is too tough to do, we try and push it for as long as we can. And what happens when a task is too easy? Well, we think it's no biggie and we can always do it later, for it will hardly take any time. I bet you would have, at some point in your life, put off that online payment for another day. Or that KYC that needed updating. Or just putting your ironed clothes in the cupboard. And then, either the task remains undone or gets added to a long list of things to do.

Think about your life and the kind of things you delay. You will realise many of them are easy to finish. And when we miss the deadline on easy things we feel so stupid. Like how could I not have done this simple thing!

Many of us are chronic procrastinators. It is as if we are only completing things because the deadline is looming. Spending the full night working just to finish that presentation. I used to be like that. I would wait until the last minute to complete a task.

Do you want to get over your habit of procrastinating? All you need to do is turn it on its head—learn to precrastinate! What's that, you may ask.

Precrastination involves completing tasks sooner rather than later, often in an effort to reduce the mental burden of having unfinished business. Unlike procrastination, which involves delaying tasks until the last minute, precrastination encourages tackling tasks head-on, even before they are due.

While procrastination is characterised by a fear of getting started, precrastination thrives on the momentum gained from immediate action.

The psychology behind precrastination is rooted in the desire for task completion and the satisfaction that comes with it. When we engage in precrastination, we experience a sense of accomplishment and reduced anxiety about looming tasks. This positive reinforcement can lead to an increased likelihood of maintaining a proactive approach to future tasks.

Want to start precrastinating? Here are three habits that will help you along.

Set micro goals. Break down larger tasks into smaller, more manageable goals. This makes it easier to take immediate action and build momentum. Micro goals are not overwhelming and hence you feel you can accomplish them without stress.

Set artificial deadlines and buffer times. While you might have to submit the project on the 20th of next month, set an artificial deadline of the 10th of the month. In this way, your mind is chasing a deadline that has enough wiggle room. The buffer time is essential for unforeseen events that might pop up. Many of us do not plan with a buffer in mind and then are in a state of panic when something unforeseen happens.

Practice the two-minute rule. If a task takes two minutes or less to complete, do it immediately. This prevents small tasks from accumulating and becoming overwhelming later. Tasks like a phone call or an email reply or even putting your clothes away—the more you delay such tasks the more mental garbage gets accumulated.

As your habit coach, I want you to be mentally free and highly productive at the same time. Precrastination is a great way of killing these two birds with one stone. No more panic attacks or the feeling of being overwhelmed just because you are procrastinating.

All you need are smaller goals, artificial deadlines and killing tasks that only need two minutes by doing them already!

Exercise

Make a list of all the things you can do in two minutes or less ... and then do them and tick them off.

____

____

____

____

____

____

____

Make a list of all the big projects and divide them in to small tasks you can schedule immediately.

____

____

____

____

____

____

____

List out the tasks that have deadlines in the coming months. Put an artificial deadline to them. Finish them before time!

____

____

____

____

____

____

____

Empty Space

Did you know that the oldest pottery discovered dates back 18,300 years? These old pot fragments were found in China. Interestingly, along with the vessels, fragments of boar, birds, turtles, fish, deer and other small mammals were also found. Clearly, these are what the people living there ate.

But something else was also discovered—a few grains of rice. It is unclear if this rice was farmed or wild rice. Especially since, scientists believe that, farming as technology was discovered many thousands of years later.

Yet humans had acquired the skill to make pots for their use. The creation of pots and vessels to carry water reflects humankind's ability to think of an immediate future. Being able to store water gave humans the ability to travel away from rivers and lakes. This allowed scope for exploration. People with pots and vessels of water were probably the travel influencers of their day.

I came across a beautiful saying, that the value of a pot is not in the walls of the pot but in the emptiness in the middle.

Let that sink in. The value of a pot is not in the actual physical material. So, it's not in its walls, the ceramic or the clay. The value of a pot or a vase comes from the hollow area. It's the nothingness in the middle, the empty space that gives it value.

Imagine if the pot was not hollowed out but made of solid clay. Technically, there would have been more material so it should have been more expensive or better. But actually it would have no value as a pot.

In order to use the pot you need it to be hollowed out.

In our modern lives, we forget this simple truth. We live lives where we think that more is always better. We don't respect empty spaces.

As your habit coach, I want you to realise that only when you create an empty space can something new come in. Only when you get rid of the old junk can you allow for something new to enter.

That is why we aim for a place of no thoughts when we meditate. We aim for nothingness. We often think that a state of no thoughts equals peace of mind. But when you listen to the Zen masters, you realise that a state of no thoughts is a way to create space.

Our minds are like the clay, the walls, the base, the structure of the vessel. Our thoughts are the contents of the vessel. Does it have water or wine?

In the same way when we look at our friends and our relationships, very often we want to change or get new people into our lives. However, in order to do that, you have to make space for them.

If you only have one parking spot, you have to sell the old car before getting a new one. You have to make space.

So your super simple habit involves identifying aspects of your life where you want to bring about a change. Then see if you have created space for that thing.

If you want to exercise for one hour a day, you need to first create a free hour for it. So learning to create space in life is the starting point for attracting things into your life.

The truth is, in order to grow, in order to be more productive. We need to create space and time. This empty time that we create is needed to flourish.

Bill Gates famously takes a full week off work, and goes away to his cabin to read and contemplate. He does this twice a year and says that his biggest breakthroughs were a result of these empty times.

Exercise

Plan out 30 minutes each day that you can spend doing nothing. Block it out in your calendar as a meeting with yourself. Spend this time thinking about your life, about your work and about yourself.

Plan when you can take a few days off, where you are not exactly on a holiday. But you are on a 'retreat' designed to create empty space in your life, welcoming new experiences.

Fail Forward

Did you know that the fear of failure can get transferred from parent to child? Studies have shown that parents transfer this fear unknowingly. Unconsciously, they move away or withhold their affection when their child fails at something.

Every time a parent reacts harshly or distances themselves, the child sees it as a big punishment. As a result, the child starts to believe that failure is unacceptable.

This becomes extremely unhealthy for the child and they can grow up believing they are not good enough. Whereas the truth is they need to fail to learn and grow. The fear of failure can be crippling. It's important that a child learns how to fail.

When we fail it is never the failure that stops our growth. It is the reaction to the failure. It is how we perceive ourselves afterwards. The things we associate our self-worth with and the way we talk to ourselves about it.

'I am useless.' 'Anyone else could have done a better job than me.' 'I should never have tried.' 'What will people think about me now?' When we start thinking like this, we become victims of our failures. We adopt the victim mentality, where we believe that we are helpless and can do nothing about it.

Very often, we just don't like to accept that we failed at something. We try disguising it. We try embellishing it. We try to show it wasn't actually a failure but an intended consequence. For example, we may make a mistake while cooking and then say we were trying something new.

The very fact that we can't accept when we fail at something should be a giant red flag! Acceptance is the first step to making a change. When was the last time you failed at something? And how did you handle it? What was your reaction?

As your habit coach, I want you to be failing at something almost every day. I want you to celebrate your failures. I want you to be so comfortable with your failures that they don't haunt you anymore. They stay in the past and you learn never to regret anything.

The key is to grow with each of your failures. Each failure should get you closer and closer to success. If you are failing over and over again without learning anything new, it is a sign that you are not learning from the experience and hence not growing.

The idea of failing forward is to understand how to grow with each failure; how to become better and better with each failure.

There are three key points to note with regard to your relationship with failure:

Accept the failure without regret. Next, identify what you have learnt from the failure without being self-deprecating. And finally find out how you can do something different the next time around. Imagine if you did this every single time that you failed. How fast you would grow from each experience.

So here's your super simple habit. The next time you fail, say to yourself: I failed at doing [X]. I learnt that I should have done [A], [B] and [C]. Next time around I will do it differently in this way [G], [H], [I].

If you distil your failure in this way, it will bring clarity.

As a practical example, I gave a talk I'm not all that proud of. So I used this technique here. I distilled my failure as: I failed at giving the best possible experience for the audience. I learnt that I should not use a hand mic, insist on the room being brighter and have my talks not too late in the evening. Next time around I shall listen to my gut and insist on these changes.

You see what I did. No self-deprecation. No self-pity. Just learning and moving forward.

Distil your failures like I did. It will only propel you towards success in the future.

Fail forward and fail fast! Each trip, is a step to success.

Exercise

Think of three recent failures and use the technique mentioned in the chapter to fail forward.

1. I failed at doing ______________________. I learnt that I should have done______________ ______________,______________________ __________, _________________________. Next time around I will do it differently in this way ____

2. I failed at doing _____________________. I learnt that I should have done______________ ______________,______________________ __________, _________________________. Next time around I will do it differently in this way ____

3. I failed at doing _____________________. I learnt that I should have done______________ ______________,______________________ __________, _________________________. Next time around I will do it differently in this way ____

Come back and use this technique anytime you fail. Hopefully you will start failing more often and learning faster!

Flights of Productivity

Did you know that only 10 to 15 per cent of the world's population has travelled by air? It's almost unbelievable to think that air travel is a luxury enjoyed by such a small proportion of people. Having said that, at any given moment in time, there are about 1.2 million people in the sky flying around the world. And this number is only growing.

Airplanes are one of my favourite modes of transportation. Why do I like air travel? Among other reasons, I have always found air travel a great way to get work done. I used to take four flights a week when I was actively working in my family business. As a market researcher, I would travel all across the country. I realised I could get a lot of work done on my flight journeys.

I see a lot of people just sitting and killing time on flights. Watching TV or watching some music videos downloaded on YouTube. But for me, this time is very valuable.

When I speak to most people and ask them why they are not as productive as they wish they were they tell me that their lives are full of distractions. They start writing an email and they receive a phone call. Or they start working on a presentation and an email arrives in their inbox. Something or the other is constantly pulling or stealing their attention.

The key to productivity is using time wisely. On a flight, your phone is off, your internet is off. There is nothing to distract you. Except for the lunch that gets served mid-way.

If you are well rested, feeling good, and high on energy, use that time to get work done. The drone of the engines on the aircraft gives you the perfect white noise to focus on your task at hand. The air conditioning is comfortable and cool. Things are perfect to work.

Here are some of my favourite ways to use this time:

> Work on documents. Do copywriting. Write blog articles. Any sort of creative writing.
>
> Write emails. The moment I land, they all get delivered.
>
> Clean up my mailbox. When I land everything syncs and I have my email optimised.
>
> Review my WhatsApp messages and find all the people who are important to me but whom I have lost touch with. Send out messages.
>
> Think. Write down ideas. Plan my next moves. This is distraction-free time and it's valuable.

Now if I have had a very long day and I am tired, or it is an early morning flight and I am still groggy, I don't work. Instead I sleep or I meditate. I am still using this time productively.

Because when I land, I will be fresh and ready to take on the day. If I had spent that time watching Netflix or YouTube I would have landed feeling sleepy and needing to rest.

This is something I learnt when travelling in first class. Almost all the passengers in the first- class cabin got on to the flight, kicked off their shoes, changed into pyjamas and went to sleep. They did not eat their meals or drink the amazing champagne. They slept the entire flight. They were using this time to rest, recover and be more productive later. A co-passenger once told me he had two board meetings to attend on landing and for him to be at his best and add value, he needed to rest and recover his energy. An interesting way to look at things, right?

So, it does not matter if yours is a thirty-minute flight or a six-hour one. Think about it as time you can use productively. On a six-hour flight, you might choose to sleep for two hours, work for two hours and then sleep for two hours. That is fine. But don't waste your time. On a thirty-minute fight, you might catch up on all your messages and email.

Use that time to be productive and take yourself ahead of everyone else. Netflix and chill or gin and tonic will show their side-effects once you land!

When I used to travel frequently I had my preflight checklist all set. I used to have my sleep mask and my earplugs in my bag. If it was an early morning flight, I would use them and sleep. I would always fly with a fully charged laptop battery. Now it is easy, I have a tablet with a keyboard, and they are surprisingly easy to use for work.

Work on your travel habits. Don't think of air time as time to kill. You can use it to make your career and business soar, while you are soaring in the sky.

Exercise

List the tools you will use in your next flight to make it productive.

____

____

____

____

____

Make a small travel kit that you take on every flight. It can contain an eye mask, an empty bottle or a folding bottle, note pad and a pen, a book to read. What is on your list?

____

____

____

____

____

Focus, Focus, Focus

Focus. The five-letter word that—if we were to master it—can make us super productive. Did you know that the origin of the word 'focus' comes from the Latin word 'focus'? Not every fun fact has to be a strange word that I cannot pronounce now, does it?

But what I find interesting is what the word 'focus' means in Latin. It means the fireplace or the hearth. When scientists started playing around with lenses they noticed how a lens would concentrate the rays of the sun on one spot, making that spot so intensely hot it could start a fire.

Hence, the focus of that lens was the spot where the sunlight's concentration was the most. It was the 'seat of the fire.' That is how we started using the word 'focus' in our everyday life to mean concentration.

I love the visualisation of the origin of this word. The seat of the fire. The seat of intensity. Yet contained in one spot.

Often listeners of my podcast reach out to me to say they aren't able to focus. They say they get distracted easily. They ask me the secret to focusing.

I don't blame them for finding it hard to focus. Being at home and working online is a big drain on the system. It takes a lot to be able to focus during Zoom meetings. Pets running around, children running around, family members asking you for things. Non-work-related things lying around and distracting you.

We are now so dependent on our phones that we have to constantly fight the temptation to keep checking the notifications. New insta alerts, new messages, notifications about what others have tweeted. There is no end to it all.

If we don't improve our focus, our productivity goes down. We do not really enjoy life. We feel tired all the time. And we live suboptimal lives.

There are three important steps and habits to form in order to improve your focus.

The first habit is to declutter your environment. Do not have things that can be a distraction lying around. Do not have toys or photographs or showpieces lying around.

Clear up the area you will be using for work. Move your phone away and keep it on a table behind you or even better, in the next room.

Think about it this way, have you ever tried to see out of a pair of spectacles that are smudged with fingerprints? It is hard to focus through a dirty glass and hence everything you see looks foggy and out of focus. If you wipe it with a cloth to clean it up, suddenly the focus improves. It is the same with our environment.

The second habit is that of planning your time and scheduling. Plan exactly how long you will be spending on a particular task. This is because while focusing on one thing, you should not have to keep wondering what is coming next, or whether or not you are doing enough. If you have decided beforehand that you need to spend thirty minutes on a task, then you don't have to wonder if you are wasting time or not.

Finally, you have to train yourself to focus on one particular thing without being distracted, like you'd train a muscle. Mothers would hate me for what I'm suggesting here, but do give it a shot. The results will be remarkable. Take a pen and make a small mark on the wall in front of your desk. It needs to be so small that it can barely be seen. I want you to sit and look at that spot only. Just keep focusing on that one spot. Do this till you get distracted. Look away for a few seconds and then start to focus on that spot again.

You will soon notice that your mind begins to quieten down. That the focus on that spot begins to get deeper and stronger. This is what we want. You are training your mind to be calm, composed and focused.

'How are you always calm and focused on Instagram lives or Zoom Workshops?' Sometimes this is posed as a question to me and sometimes as a compliment. People say that they enjoy seeing that calm. The truth is that I am completely focused in that moment with the viewers. There is no place else to be.

As your habit coach I want to see this calm in you too. Train yourself to focus on that one spot on the wall in front of your work desk. Focus till you see that dot and nothing but that dot. Soon the world around you will disappear, your mind will quieten and become sharper. And you'll be able to start a fire of creativity.

Exercise

Imagine a perfect workstation for yourself, a place free of distraction. Describe it in the space below. Once you do, you'll have a clear idea of what a distraction free work zone should look like for you.

Make a plan for your focused work time.

Practise focusing at a dot on the wall for a minimum of three minutes. Write down how many minutes you could focus on the dot the first time around. Write down how many minutes you could focus for after seven days.

Day 1: ________________________

Day 7: ________________________

How Not to Be a Super(wo)man: Be a CEO instead

Here's a fun fact: Sumer in Mesopotamia is the first place we see the economic principle of division of labour recorded in history. This is a key turning point in the history of humankind.

Division of labour is one of the most important concepts for our society to exist. Without it, we would have perished before reaching the age of cave men.

The idea is that each person in a community plays a specific role. Each person does something different and vital to the functioning of the society. A farmer grows the crops, an engineer designs the buildings, a plumber fixes the water supply—you get the drift, right?

In hunter-and-gatherer societies, the division of labour existed based on gender. The women would gather berries and roots, and take care of the children. The men would hunt and build huts. Within these, there would be specialisations as well. For instance, one member of the tribe would be responsible for the drums and the music on a hunt.

The Dutch were once the most powerful people in the world. The key advantage they had over other countries was with regard to shipbuilding. Other countries did not have specialised roles in the ship-building process; the builders would do anything that was needed. The Dutch shipbuilders had very specialised roles. One person specialised in the sail and hence developed his own unique abilities and techniques. Thus they were able to advance very quickly.

The idea of division of labour is a very powerful one in the corporate world. Which is why we have so many roles and hierarchies. If we work in companies, we are automatically a part of this division of labour.

Where we fail to understand this concept is in our personal lives. We do not realise that we can use the principle of the division of labour to make our lives better. Instead, we try and do everything ourselves. We become the Jack of all trades. This leads to failure. I once worked with an entrepreneur who was running a very successful start-up. She insisted on running the business, cleaning the house, washing and ironing the clothes, cooking the meals and doing everything herself. She had a grown-up son and a husband. This poor woman was so burnt out. She was constantly trying to juggle everything and then when it did not work out, she felt like a failure.

Her health—both physical and mental—took the toll.

As her habit coach, my first goal was to explain to her that she does not need to behave like a superwoman and do everything herself. That it is okay for her to ask for help and divide up all the tasks that need to be done. Her daily habits were restricting her growth and potential.

I made her list all the tasks she did in a day. Then next to each task, I made her put a mark. 'C' on tasks that were her core competencies and ones only she could do. 'E' on tasks she enjoyed doing. 'O' on tasks that could be outsourced. She soon realised that 75 per cent of the list could be outsourced and that she did not need to be doing those things.

She asked her husband to take care of the home accounting, which he happily did. She asked her son to help with the laundry, which he grudgingly did. She enjoyed cooking so I let her keep that task.

Soon she hired an Executive Assistant to help her with the office tasks. And as soon as she divided up all these tasks her life became so much easier. She was no longer burnt out. She was better at her work and could grow the business. But what she really thanked me for was her family life. She used to believe that doing all the home tasks would make her a better mother and wife. However, in the new system, she had more time and energy to spend with the family and this improved her relationship with them tremendously.

This is the power of division of labour in our personal lives. We need to use this principle to have a more fulfilling life. Let others handle things that are not in your scope of expertise. Focus on the things you are good at or enjoy doing. Hire help if you need to. Most of the time the value you get from hiring someone is far more than the cost of hiring them.

So your super simple habit starts by making a list of all the things you are doing every day. Next to each item, put a 'C' for core competencies, an 'O' for outsource and an 'E' for the things you enjoy.

Continue to do the C and E activities and outsource all the Os.

Remember you are the CEO of your life so act like one!

Exercise

Make a 'C' list of all your core competencies, things only you can do.

____

____

____

____

____

List all your 'E' items, things you enjoy doing.

____

____

____

____

____

List all your 'O' items, things you can outsource.

____

____

____

____

____

How Will You Measure Work?

Time management is a buzzword in the workplace. Did you know that the whole idea of time management is a product of the Industrial Revolution? During the Industrial Revolution the physical manufacturing of products started taking place at huge volumes.

During this time, companies hired people to make the processes as efficient as possible. The aim was to maximise the output of a person. This led to factories working 24X7, with people working in shifts to get as many final products as possible.

The output always had a maximum possible number. For example, a man could only produce a hundred products in a nine-hour shift.

As a result, time spent was equal to work done. The more time you spent the more work you did. The less time you spent working the less work you did. It was a completely logical way of thinking about work output in manufacturing.

This style of thinking naturally crept into our education system as well. This was understandable since our modern style of education was created during the Industrial Revolution. Our modern education system was designed to create workers in factories and administrative offices.

Think back to when you were in school. How did you measure how hard you studied? It was always by the amount of time you spent studying. You measured your exam preparation by the number of hours you'd spent studying the previous day.

You would say, 'I was studying till two in the morning.' A friend of yours would say, 'I only got four hours to study, I am failing for sure.' And then that liar would get the highest marks in the exam!

In our modern workplace, we have replaced physical manufacturing with intellectual manufacturing. We are creating software and ideas. We are coming up with branding strategies, marketing plans and so on.

And we all know that one can spend four hours working and still come up with zero output. We get distracted by our phones. Or we are mentally down because of something that happened at home, or because of a fight we had with a loved one. We can spend all day trying to work and get nothing done.

And then there are other times when you feel like a superhero—when you manage to complete all the work that you need to do in just one hour, or when you have that spark of an idea for a new marketing plan.

Think about it. When your boss gives you a task to do, they expect you to complete it with a certain amount of quality. They don't care if it takes you ten hours or eight hours to finish it. Of course, they'll be happier if you did the same work faster. In our modern life, however, work cannot be measured in terms of time spent.

Narayana Murthy, the founder of Infosys, one of the biggest tech companies in the world, was in the news recently for his statement that the youth need to work seventy hours a week. That would make for ten hours of work every day—or twelve hours if you follow a six-day week.

This caused a big uproar and many articles were written about work–life balance and on how companies are exploiting employees. I was interviewed by a few newspapers and news channels about this topic.

Whether Mr Murthy is right or not, is not for me to judge. As your habit coach, I'm more concerned about making your lives better. And all I can say about measuring our work by the time we spend doing it is: it's silly. We need to measure our work differently.

I have worked with many clients who would spend twelve hours a day working. However, effectively, they didn't spend twelve hours working. Most of them were incredibly distracted. Picking up the phone to check a message or receive a call would lead to long, unplanned reel-scrolling breaks.

When we calculated we realised, they were probably working for only four hours out of those twelve. Imagine, only a third of the so-called work hours were being spent on work!

And I know you feel this too. I know this is probably happening to you as well, unless you have created a set of habits for your work life.

You are not a factory worker, building something with your hands. You are someone creating something with your mind. And our minds get distracted and wander all over the place. We need to create the right productivity habits for ourselves.

I want you to start observing how you work. Are you focused? Do you get distracted? How long can you keep your attention on one task?

The truth is that you do not need to work seventy hours a week if you learn to work efficiently. Most of us only need about six hours of focused work a day. Imagine if you finished all your work in six hours. You could spend the remaining three hours on things you want to do, like working on a hobby or a passion project, or spending time with family and friends.

If you ask me, this is true work-life balance—to work more efficiently so one can find balance in life again.

So how much of the day are you actually working? Get into the habit of measuring your time and productivity and you will then be able to improve it. Spend less time working but get more done in the end.

Exercise

Get a note book and divide your work day into about five big daily tasks that you do.

For example, ABC project, marketing, admin, meetings, networking and so on.

Now track how much time is actually spent on the tasks. Break the time down into 15 minute increments, so that you are more conscious of time wasted.

Be mindful of how much time is wasted and how much is spent on focused work.

If Only We'd Stopped at Smoke Signals: The Communication Burnout

In *Castaway*, the character played by Tom Hanks is stranded on an island. In his attempts to be rescued, he creates fire to send a smoke signal.

Smoke signals are one of the oldest ways of long-distance communication. Their earliest known use was along the Great Wall of China, around 900 BCE, where soldiers would use it to communicate attacks from enemy tribes. Since the wall was so long, it would be impossible to defend all of it without a way to communicate.

In 150 BCE the Greek historian Polybius devised a way to communicate alphabets and words using smoke and fire. He turned all of the letters into numbers and used that to spell the words.

While in this age of gadgets and gizmos, smoke signals may sound outdated, the fact is we still use them for important historical information. When a new pope is being elected, black smoke is let out of the chimney to signal a hung or failed vote while white smoke is used to signal a successful election of the next pope.

Today, it's so easy for us to communicate. We have mobile phones and the internet. But I grew up in the era of public telephones and phones with big dials on them. Unlike today, when our phones have become like extensions of our hands, in the time of landlines and pay phones, our days were peaceful. You wouldn't get more than three or four calls in a day, and the calls were to do with family and friends inquiring about our well-being. There couldn't have been any work calls on those phones!

That was also the time of phone directories. An annual phone book would get delivered at home every year, which contained listings of all phone numbers. I remember looking up the phone numbers of girls my friends might have a crush on. I'd guess which number could be theirs based on their last name and the area they lived in. Today, we all talk about privacy, but back then, clearly there was no concept of it! But like I said, phone calls were rare and we mostly met in person to communicate.

Compare that with today's world. On an average a thirty-five-year-old sends a hundred messages a day. The younger generations are messaging far more. Add to it emails and DMs and Snapchat. Not to forget, the endless spam phone calls. And then the hours spent scrolling through Instagram, Twitter and Facebook.

We may not be conscious of it, but each post we see on social media is a message we are picking up.

In this hyper-connected world, we are all suffering from something called communications fatigue. Also known as communication burnout, it is a state of exhaustion. It decreases one's effectiveness due to prolonged and excessive communication. This can happen in various contexts, including work, relationships and online interactions.

In our modern digital age, communication has become more constant and all-pervasive than ever before. While our modern communication tools offer numerous benefits in terms of connectivity and convenience, they can also lead to a range of negative effects, including communication burnout.

Here are three negative effects.

Constant connectivity gives the feeling of being connected 24/7. It makes us feel constantly 'switched on'. Our human biology was not designed for this kind of activity. We were designed to be switched off from time to time in order to recharge. When we are constantly on, we begin to feel tired and depressed.

The blurring of boundaries is another problem with being so connected. We often do not realise when work stops and our personal life starts. You might switch your laptop off but a work message from your colleague on WhatsApp is still work. When I first started working we did not have laptops and at that time, taking your work home meant lugging around huge files and paperwork. Now everything is constantly with us in the cloud.

We now expect immediate responses. This is the worst outcome of new technology. Our style of communication has killed our ability to be patient. We want to know everything as soon as we ask. This puts us under pressure to reply immediately even when we do not have the energy or the mind space to do so.

Communication burnout is a real thing millions of people are suffering from. Every time you look at your phone in dread expecting a message from someone—it's a sign of communication burnout. Every time you feel tired and fling your phone away—again, it's a sign of communication burnout.

As your habit coach, I want you to be in control of your communication and not feel overwhelmed by it. Here are a few habits you can use to prevent such a burnout.

First, we need to learn to draw our boundaries. You do not need to reply to everyone who messages you instantly. You do not need to make yourself available to the world all the time. When I was growing up the polite thing to do was answer the phone before the second ring and always maintain communication. This was because communication was expensive back then and only important things were communicated. Today it is free and hence it is abused. You need to create a system where you do not answer calls or messages when you are busy or resting or with your family. Keeping your phone on DND, or do not disturb, is a great way to maintain that boundary. Another great way is to not look at work emails outside of work hours and reply to official WhatsApp messages only when you are in work mode.

The second habit is to keep aside two hours in the day when your phone is on airplane mode. No one can reach you and you cannot do any endless scrolling. I do this one hour after I wake up and one hour before going to bed. This way I maintain my sanity and moments of peace from the endless stream of communication.

The third habit is to check your email only twice a day. When you do this, you are not distracted by emails coming in through the day when you are focusing on preparing a presentation deck. For instance, my phone is off and my emails deactivated on my laptop when I am working on my podcast or when I am writing my books.

As your habit coach I want you to be mindful of your communication. Are you oversharing? Are you spending too much time thinking about other people's problems? You need to make a conscious change.

Even our phones need to take a break and get charged from time to time. We, too, must learn to draw boundaries and recharge our batteries.

Exercise

Look back at the last week and note down five instances when you overshared or over communicated. How would you handle it differently in the future?

____

____

____

____

Decide a time during the day, when you will put the phone away or in airplane mode so that you are not tempted to look at your phone and communicate. List out the things you could focus on during this time.

____

____

____

____

Switch off email notifications on your phone. And decide on two times during the day when you will check your email. You do not have to answer it every second of the day.

____

____

____

____

It Doesn't Have to Be a Struggle: Transitional Habits to a Good Day at Work

How many years have you spent at your current workplace? Or let me ask: what has been your longest stint at an organisation? The Guinness World Record for the longest career in the same company is held by someone who worked at a company for—believe it or not—eighty-four years and nine days!

Walter Orthmann was born in Brazil in 1922. In 1938—on 17 January, to be precise—he began working at Industrias Renaux S.A. He was only fifteen years old at that time. It was in 2022 that his name entered the Guinness Book of World Records. He was already a hundred years old then. (In August 2024, Orthmann passed away.)

When Orthmann was fourteen, his mother took him to find a job. He was the eldest of five kids and back then there were no laws against child labour. He started his career as a shipping assistant and, in the course of time, was transferred to sales and finally became a manager.

I love learning from people who have lived over a hundred years. They have a very different perspective on life, especially around work, family and happiness.

In today's world, where work is seen in such a toxic way, how did Walter survive? There is a quote by Walter that I wish to share with you: 'When we do what we like, we don't see the time go by, I don't do much planning, nor care much about tomorrow. All I care about is that tomorrow will be another day in which I will wake up, get up, exercise, and go to work; you need to get busy with the present, not the past or the future. Here and now is what counts. So, let's go to work!'

Such beautiful advice. Focus on the day you have in front of you. Do not dwell on the past or worry about the future. Just focus on the day and do what you like doing.

So, is there a way we can begin having good days at work?

Most of us snooze our alarms in the morning and go back to sleep. It's like we're trying our best to avoid the day. But the fact is: the day doesn't go anywhere. All that snoozing the alarm does is give us a late start. And when we finally get out of bed it is a mad rush to get ready and leave for work.

In the process, we have fought with our family, argued with our partner, dealt with our kid's temper tantrums, spilled the morning coffee on our clothes—or, if we are unlucky enough, then even dealt with all of this in one morning. And all this before we've reached the office.

In office, we have a million things waiting for us. We have angry clients and fires to put out. All this stress piles up. It is no wonder we find our work lives toxic. It is because we carry our personal lives into the workplace and our workplace into our personal lives.

The best way to have a good day is by being in control of your day.

What we need are transitioning habits—a set of habits we should follow in the car, bus or train while commuting to work. And we need to create a routine for arriving at work.

The goal of transitioning habits is to transition from 'home mode' to 'work mode'. If we don't do that, the lines between our work and personal lives remain blurred, and we end up bringing our home problems to work. This hampers our productivity at work.

One of my favourite transition habits in the car, on my way to work, is to send a message to the people at home. This can be your family or your partner or your kids. Saying something sweet and simple like, 'I am on my way to work, I love you and I will see you in the evening soon.' Send this on days you have had an argument with them or even on days that were uneventful. The goal of this habit is to switch your mind off the home and get into focus mode at work.

When you reach office follow these three habits.

First, set your bags down and go to the pantry, and get yourself a hot beverage. On the way to the pantry, speak to your colleagues. Then sit down at your desk and write on a pad: 'I am grateful to have a job and come to work.' Most of us take this for granted but we know so many people who are unemployed or have lost their jobs. Continue writing on that same sheet what you want to achieve by having this job: you want to buy a house or become the CEO, it can be anything. And the last habit before you get to the daily work is to write down what you want to achieve today. How will today be productive?

Only once you have completed these three habits should you open your laptop or check your email or get into your first meeting.

You will notice that I am deliberately slowing down your process of starting work. This is because I want you to begin work in a calm, relaxed and controlled manner.

If you do these habits, you will have a good day—a productive day! And work will never be something you want to run away from.

Exercise

Create a list of transition habits for when you move from home mode to work mode.

1. ______________________________________

2. ______________________________________

3. ______________________________________

Create a list of transition habits for when you move from work mode to home mode.

1. ______________________________________

2. ______________________________________

3. ______________________________________

It's You Versus Your Phone

A fun fact: our phones have a minimum operating temperature. If the temperature drops below that, our phone stops working.

For the iPhone the minimum operating temperature is –4 to 0 degrees centigrade. So why does the phone freeze along with your fingers?

The issue lies with the battery. According to *Time* magazine, as the temperature drops, the internal resistance increases. The phone battery relies on chemical reactions to work. Cold prevents or slows down these reactions from taking place.

I remember trying to take a picture when it was –15 degrees and my fully charged phone showed me a 7 per cent battery and then died. Luckily, I had just enough charge to take pictures on the top of Mount Kilimanjaro.

It's funny but when we go for these high-altitude treks where the night temperatures drop below zero, we have to keep batteries close to our body. Phones and cameras need to join us in the sleeping bag so that they remain warm and maintain a charge.

Even at our warm sea level, phone batteries do not last very long these days. Think about how often we have to stop and charge them through the day. We have a charging cable stashed at home and work—not to forget the car!

I remember a funny meme that I came across a while ago that showed how phones evolved from being attached to the walls to cordless phones, then mobile phones. It seems now we are back to being attached to the walls with our smartphones needing to be charged all the time!

Our phone batteries do not last long because we use our phone so much. We spend close to three hours a day on our phones, scrolling and surfing, liking and commenting. We spend our time looking at a white screen.

Often, people ask me what my bad habits are and I tell them that I am addicted to my phone. People find it amusing that I too have bad habits even though I am a habit coach. But it's true. Phones are so hard to resist. It's such an uphill task trying to break this habit. I have tried so many different methods, many of which did help me a great deal.

This piece isn't about those methods though. I want to talk instead about how I like challenges. I like them because they turn a task into a game. You can challenge yourself to do hard things and you can also challenge your friends.

The challenge is to see how long you can make your phone last on one full charge. Yes, you heard me. How many days do you think you can make your phone go on for?

These are called endurance challenges. You have to become ultra mindful. Use the phone only when you need to. A mistake or an unnecessary conversation can dramatically lessen the battery.

There are so many benefits to using your battery as a measure of how well you have performed. It's instant feedback; you have a percentage right there. The phone is constantly using up data and its charge even when you are not using it actively. This will make you cognisant of all the background activities you can stop.

For example, the phone checking weather data. If you are in Mumbai the weather is hot. Just hot. You don't need the phone to tell you that.

I noticed the battery challenge made me hyper aware every time I opened Instagram or WhatsApp. I also realised just how many unnecessary YouTube videos I was watching.

Now, if you are like me and want to cheat a little or, let's say, optimise the settings and usage as much as you can, here are a few tools you can use:

Adjust the screen brightness to as dark as possible. Put the auto-brightness off.

Move all the distracting apps, like Instagram, YouTube, Facebook and WhatsApp, away from the home screen into a separate folder.

Make sure Wi-Fi, Bluetooth and GPS, all are switched off.

Put off auto-rotation of the screen.

Put off active wallpapers.

The next two are very important:

Put the phone on airplane mode when you are working or when not using it. Putting the phone in airplane mode prolongs the charge. It also keeps distractions at bay. So, the airplane mode is not just for flights. It's for everyday use when you're trying to fly through life and distractions. And here's a bonus: your phone in airplane mode will also reduce your exposure to EMF radiation.

Lastly, put all notifications off. Notifications will light up the screen and drain the charge. But what's worse is that they draw you to check the phone and see what you missed. Notifications are other people stealing your time.

So your super simple habit to fight phone addiction is to simply not charge your phone every day. See how many days you can go on a single charge. I bet as of now it's probably one day if not half a day!

Find the tools you need to maintain this for as long as possible. Challenge a few of your friends. The rule is simple. How long can your phone last on one charge? Use every trick in the book. It will be hard in the beginning. But I can guarantee that it will be worth it. You'll find yourself claiming your time back and your productivity will soar with this simple act of not feeding the distractions.

Exercise

Cut down all the battery drains mentioned in this chapter.

Take the challenge. Write below, 'I accept the battery challenge.'

____

____

____

Do this challenge over a week and write down how many hours you were able to make the battery last on your phone.

1. ______________________________________
2. ______________________________________
3. ______________________________________
4. ______________________________________
5. ______________________________________
6. ______________________________________
7. ______________________________________

Lakshya and Lakshmi

Among the gods and goddesses that Hindus pray to is goddess Lakshmi. While we think of her as the goddess of wealth, and the Hindus especially pray to her on the day of Diwali, here's a fun fact: the name Lakshmi was most likely derived from the word lakS, which means to perceive or observe. This, of course, is the word that transforms into 'lakshya,' the Hindi word for aim or goal.

So, goddess Lakshmi brings you not money but your lakshyas or goals.

I realised this connection when I was attending a puja for Maa Lakshmi. During the puja, everyone was focusing on money. As part of the puja, we draw feet at the entrance. These feet, pointing inwards, are said to symbolise goddess Lakshmi entering the house.

Everyone at the puja was singing along to '*Mere ghar aao Lakshmi Maa*,' which translates to 'Come to my home, Mother Lakshmi.'

This is when the habit coach in me woke up. I realised that if we don't have a clear goal or lakshya, what will Lakshmi Maa come to our home and do? If she is the bringer of goals, what goal of yours will she bless?

Having been a habit coach long enough, I know most people have no clear goals. Most people have vague goals, like 'I want lots of money' or 'I want to live next to a beach' or 'I want a hot boyfriend/girlfriend.'

These statements are meaningless. What is 'a lot of money'? Is it a hundred dollars, 100 million dollars or 100 billion dollars? You can live next to the beach in a one-bedroom apartment, in a villa or homeless on a bench next to the beach.

We often pray for things we are unclear about and then wonder why they do not become a reality. The reason is that we do not know what we truly want.

So let's do some goal setting today. Get a paper and pen and answer the following questions. You may have multiple goals for different aspects of your life and that is fine. For now, choose just one thing that you want to accomplish and write it down mentioning the following details.

What do you want to achieve? Give as much detail as possible.

Quantify it. Put a number to your goal; don't leave it abstract.

By when do you want to achieve it? Put a deadline to your goal.

What is the emotion associated with achieving your goal? Is it happiness, excitement, sense of achievement?

So your goal might look like this: I am so excited to stay in my white-coloured five-bedroom pool villa by the beach in Miami by May 2027.

I know this will be very hard for you to do, especially if this is your first time setting a goal like this. It takes a lot of patience and understanding. You will really need to sit with your goals and spend time with them to gain clarity.

I suggest thinking about them first thing in the morning after you wake up.

Once you have your goals think about what you will need to achieve these goals:

The resources: money, time, land and so on.

People who can help you achieve them.

Skills you will need; for example, negotiation skills.

The next thing I want you to do is to make a plan or a strategy for achieving these goals. What are the steps you need to take to get there? For example, I need to earn X amount of money to be able to buy this home. I need to learn four new skills to be able to charge more money. I need to invest this money in XYZ.

Then start taking the first steps towards these goals. Start acting on the goals. Create momentum towards them. It is this clarity of action that will bring you the best results.

So your super simple habit of achieving anything starts by having a clear goal for yourself. You can have twenty goals for twenty different aspects of your life–health, work, relationships, etc. Once you have clear goals, identify what you will need to achieve them. And then make a clear plan to accomplish them.

I can guarantee that the difference between people who achieve things in life and those who do not can be gauged by the clarity of their goals.

And only once you have finished the above steps and started taking action should you start praying.

Exercise

What is your goal? ______________________________
____

What do you want to achieve? Give as much detail as possible.

____

____

____

Quantify it. Put a number to your goal; don't leave it abstract.

____

____

____

By when do you want to achieve it? Put a deadline to your goal.

____

____

____

What is the emotion associated with achieving your goal? Is it happiness, excitement or a sense of achievement?

____

____

What do you need to achieve this goal?

The resources:

____

____

____

People who can help you:

____

____

____

Skills you will need:

____

____

____

Mind Mapping

Did you know that our brains are wired to make connections and not just store data like a hard drive does? In fact, if we think of our brain as just a sophisticated computer hard drive or a memory disk, we are missing the bigger picture. P.K. Anokhin speaks about this.

Anokhin was a prominent Russian scientist. Back in the mid-1900s, he made significant contributions to cybernetics and psychophysiology. He said that the brain likes to work on the basis of associations; it will connect every idea, memory or piece of information to tens, hundreds and even thousands of other ideas and concepts.

It's like a free-floating jigsaw puzzle of information, each piece morphing and dancing to form a complete picture.

The faster you can grow these connections the better. More connections give you the opportunity to increase your creative potential. More connections give you the ability to remember and recall information faster. In which case we should be doing everything in our ability to try and feed this connecting ability of our brain.

However, most of us are taught that in order to keep notes and ideas, we have to form lists, paragraphs and bullet points. Think about this: our school books were all paragraphs and had to be read from top to bottom, from left to right. There was no scope of creating connections there. We were taught to note down the important points; we made lists.

At work all our presentations are in the form of bullet points. How can you possibly connect an idea from slide 23 to slide 140 to form something creative this way?

Clearly, we aren't all using our brains in an optimal manner. We aren't supporting its function. We aren't boosting it in any way. It's no wonder studying and learning back in school was so hard. We didn't give the brain an easy way of memory recall. The other day, on Instagram, I put up a picture of me working. I had these circles on a page with stuff written in them. In the description I asked if everyone else uses this technique called mind mapping. I was shocked because lots of people wrote in asking what it is!

For me, mind mapping has become second nature. I used it while studying for my MBA. When I started working, it was the first thing that was taught to me. Ormax Consultants, my family business, works in the area of understanding consumer behaviour. We deal with a lot of data and information. So we found mind maps were the best tools to use when making a presentation to our clients.

What is a mind map? The idea was popularised by Tony Buzan many decades ago. He defined it as a 'Graphical technique for visualising connections between several ideas or pieces of information. Each idea or fact is written down and then linked by lines or curves to its major or minor (or following or previous) idea or fact, thus creating a web of relationships.'

It's basically a sheet of paper on which you put down all your thoughts in a stream of consciousness. Each thought you put in a circle. Now start connecting circles and ideas together. You will soon realise that there are so many different ways to view the same information.

Mind mapping dramatically boosts creativity, as you can now connect ideas. You can create a new way to look at an old problem.

If you are a student, mind mapping is the perfect tool for you to remember data and information. This is because the mind likes to remember things visually.

Pro tip: use different colours for different ideas and sets. Draw little stars and other things around important points so you remember them. I now use one of those pens that have four different ink colours, so it's easy to change the colour and highlight something.

The bottom line is that mind maps are the most important tool you can have in your productivity arsenal. I have studied them extensively and worked with them extensively. They are a must have productivity habit.

So your super simple habit for increasing the efficiency of your brain is to start using mind maps. Don't make linear lists, instead start drawing your bubbles or circles and start inserting thoughts and ideas into them.

Get yourself a packet of colourful pens. Sit down with a blank sheet of paper and start practising mind maps for your notes.

You'll appreciate their recall value and their positive impact on your productivity.

Exercise

Watch two YouTube videos on how to mind map. Make your own practice mind map in the space below.

Newton's Law of Motion (and Productivity)

Isaac Newton. What is the first thing that pops in your head when you hear that name? Gravity, right? But there's more to Sir Isaac Newton. And I'm not even talking about the laws of motion!

Did you know that Newton had predicted that the end of the world would not happen before 2060? So we have another thirty-six years at least! The reason why Newton predicted this was because he had a passion for alchemy.

You can think of alchemy as the science that existed before chemistry became more formalised. Alchemists had two great obsessions. The first was to turn base metals or worthless metals into precious metals like gold and silver. The second obsession was to find an elixir for life—something that could make us live forever.

This side of Newton was kept well hidden from the public for a long time, to safeguard his reputation. He did not want that people associate him with alchemy rather than the work he did in mathematics and physics. In fact, he wrote more on alchemy and religion than he did on mathematics and science. After his death, his family kept these books hidden. They probably feared that those writings would tarnish the work for which he is known.

This is where the prediction of the end of the world comes into play. Newton spent time poring over the Bible and concluded that the apocalypse would happen after 2060.

My focus here is not on Newton's religious beliefs but on Newton's law of momentum. Momentum is the force that exists in an object. The more momentum an object has the harder it is to stop.

It takes a lot of energy to get to the desired momentum. However, once that momentum is achieved. It takes very little energy to keep it going. Think of a train or a car. It takes a lot of energy to start a train and a car. But once it is cruising, it keeps moving with very little effort.

This is why our fuel consumption is so low on the highways. We get 20 kilometres per litre on the highways, but in the city it drops all the way down to 7 kilometres per litre. This is because the car's momentum keeps it going on highways. It needs to burn very little fuel there to keep moving.

When we are driving in the city, we have to constantly stop and start, stop and start. There are traffic signals but also traffic jams. Someone decides to randomly jump lanes in front of us or a cow decides to stroll across the road. And all these make us slow down, they make us stop.

When we have come to a complete stop there is inertia to start moving again. Inertia is another Newtonian principle. Energy and fuel are needed to overcome inertia and gain momentum.

The principles of inertia and momentum apply to our work lives too.

You must have experienced days when you are so deep into your work that you have forgotten what time it is. You have achieved far more than what you would have normally done. There were no distractions and you were flying on the productivity highway. You aren't tired because it does not use up a lot of your energy.

But now let's look at a normal day of work when we come home very tired. Most of that day would have been spent juggling many different things. Firefighting a problem. Replying to a sudden and urgent email. Talking to friends about yesterday's football game. Scrolling on social media.

All of these things are like the red lights, the traffic jams and the cows on the road of productivity. It takes so much effort and energy to keep starting and stopping by all these distractions in our daily lives.

We must learn to gain momentum in our work days. The way I do this is by finding long stretches of time where I can work uninterrupted and without distractions. This is when I gain my daily momentum. This is like taking the productivity highway. My morning time is one such slot where I can work for a few hours uninterrupted.

Then I get into the daily traffic of life. It is like entering a city after being on a highway. Once I have dealt with all the distractions, I get back on the highway for the final stretch.

When I have gained momentum, I protect it fiercely. I make sure there are no apps on my phone that can distract me with notifications. I keep my phone away from me. I even switch off my email application.

I prepare myself for these sessions by using the washroom and getting myself a nice hot mug of coffee or tea before I begin. This is because little breaks can kill the momentum.

However, our productivity is not just a daily activity. Momentum exists over a week, a month and a year as well. Ask a salesperson and they will tell you that momentum exists in their work as well. If they get a few sales close to each other that momentum begins to carry through the whole month. However, if there is a break or holiday in the middle, that momentum crashes.

So your super simple habit starts by thinking about your productivity like Newton. Your work has momentum. If you want to be productive you need to learn how to maintain that momentum. The more momentum you have the less effort you will need to get things done.

Start by thinking about your work like driving on the highway or in traffic. No one likes driving in traffic. So clear the distractions that can slow you down. And be fiercely protective about your momentum.

Exercise

Make a list of all the things that kill your momentum on a daily basis. And next to them write down what you can do to clear them out (yes, you can even include your chatty office colleague in this list).

____

____

____

____

____

____

Make a list of all the things that destroy your weekly, monthly and yearly momentum. And what can you do about it (think festivals and other yearly activities).

____

____

____

____

____

____

Next Five Moves

Do you play chess? It's a game of strategy. On the last move, before knocking off the opponent's king, the winner exclaims: checkmate! Did you know that the origin of this word is Persian?

While the word 'checkmate' doesn't make sense, the original Persian word was 'Shah maat'. 'Shah' means king and 'maat' means dead. So it literally meant the king is dead, which makes sense.

I played chess while I was in school but was terrible at it. I must have used the expression, 'checkmate' maybe once or twice. I was so bad at the game that I stopped playing it.

The game of chess requires one key skill, a skill I certainly lacked then. Most chess grandmasters can visualise the next ten moves and plan for the next five. Across the board, the best players in the world all say almost the same thing. Five moves ahead is what they are planning.

I could not plan five moves ahead. My brain would hurt just at the thought of it. I would simply wait for my opponent's move and react to it. So, essentially, I was always playing a reactive game. Or, to put it differently, I was always playing someone else's game.

Most of us go through life like that. Playing a reactive game reacting to what others are doing. We compare ourselves to them, copy them. This is why we fail.

We don't plan our life and so we are swept away by the lives of others. We follow the crowd.

A majority of us end up planning our vacations but not our work, relationships or health paths. We end up thinking about these things only when we are having our annual appraisals at work, or our relationship starts failing, or when there's a health scare.

We should learn from the chess grandmasters. They clearly know something we don't. They are visualising the next ten moves. They are envisioning their goal, their destination. Where they ultimately want to reach. However, those ten moves have too many variables. What if the opponent does not play a move according to plan? What if something strange happens in the fourth move?

That is why they only plan the next five moves at a time. If things don't go according to plan, the move changes.

Imagine, if we could visualise the goal for the year. Each aspect of our life could have its own goal. What would those goals look like? Work goals, relationship goals, health goals, financial goals, etc.

I want you to write down your next five moves for each of these goals. The next five moves for your work goals might be:

Learn a new skill.

Make a presentation to the team showcasing the new skill.

Ask the boss for a tougher project to use this skill.

Help the boss in their work.

Ask the boss for a raise.

Each aspect of your life has steps that can be taken to achieve the goal. You need to spend time thinking about these steps and then take them.

If you cannot plan the next five moves, you will be like what I was in school. Never winning in chess, or in this case the game of life.

So your super simple habit starts by sitting down with a piece of paper and planning your next five moves for each aspect of your life. Be very clear how you define these moves. Don't be vague. Put a measurable quantity for the steps so that you can be as clear about them as possible.

Then take action. If a grandmaster planned the moves in his head and never played them, it would be such a waste.

It will be difficult to do this at first. You might feel like your brain is exploding with all the thinking. But that is good. It will get easier over time. Stop playing a reactive game to someone else's life and start winning in yours.

Exercise

Plan your next five moves at work.

____

____

____

____

____

Plan the next five moves in your relationship/ friendship.

____

____

____

____

____

Plan the next five moves in your health journey.

____

____

____

____

____

Open Tabs vs Deep Work

Do you realise how much time you spend surfing the internet every day? If you do your surfing on your mobile phones, the weekly screen time report will give you a break-up of the amount of time spent on various social media apps as well as on generally surfing the internet on the browser. Of course we can also be surfing on our laptops.

A study conducted on employees of a few companies revealed that they spent an average of two to three hours every day surfing about topics that were not related to their work.

That's three hours every single day on something that's unproductive and distracting. What's more, there have even been studies that show a link between compulsive surfing and the shrinking of the prefrontal cortex of the brain, the centre responsible for decision-making.

Right now there isn't enough information for the cause of this shrinking. One possible explanation could be that we rely on the internet to answer all our questions, make all the decisions for us. We may not realise this, but in essence, we are outsourcing what the prefrontal cortex was designed to do for us.

Interestingly, surfing can be very stressful and tiring. Have you ever felt drained after a long bout of surfing the internet? This is because we spend a lot of time switching in between streams of information. Every time we switch, we leave a thought incomplete. These incomplete thoughts add up and can be a cause for stress.

We are always looking for something better. Always searching and never satisfied. It can become an endless pursuit. Watching videos or reels is a classic example of this. You start researching the role of cortisol in the body and one hour later, you find yourself watching kittens fall off tables. Ha, I knew you would relate to this one!

One classic way we do this is by using multiple tabs on our browser. On an average, people have between ten and fifteen tabs open at any given point of time. Some super tab users have over twenty! In fact twenty is the maximum number allowed in Google Chrome. You can of course overwrite this default setting.

I remember the dark ages before internet browser tabs. We had to open new windows each time. And the moment we did, the computer just got slower and slower. When tabs were launched it was a relief. What a brilliant idea, we thought.

And it is indeed a brilliant idea till we start seeing the adverse impact on our productivity.

It's the same as multitasking. We may think that we are being smart and handling multiple things at the same time. However, there is no such thing as multitasking. There is only task switching. And every time we task switch there is a cost associated with it.

Having twenty tabs open is like having twenty tasks that are happening simulateneously, at any given point of time. Twenty tabs mean twenty things you have left half done. It means twenty things that are distracting you.

When you finally retire for the night, leaving those tabs open on your laptop to tackle the next day, the fact is that those tabs remain open in your mind as well, at a subconscious level. The next day when you start the computer and all twenty tabs open up, the brain sees it as twenty things to do and has a stress response. Notice your breathing the next time your computer loads with so many tabs open. Don't you feel anxious?

Don't worry, I am not dissing tab browsing. This isn't about tabs being bad. Instead, it's about identifying a smarter way of using them. Tabs are great and essential for research and being creative. They let you explore and build up new ideas. Feeding off information from one website, mixing it with another and thinking of a beautiful way to present it. Tabs, however, cause havoc when we are implementing, using, creating or producing the ideas we have discovered.

For example, tabs are absolutely essential while I am researching information for my podcast episodes, doing fact-checking or organising data. However, once I start writing and working on the script these tabs distract me. For it is not the time for me to explore. Rather, this is the time for me to put my nose to the ground and work in a focused manner. It is called deep work.

During your deep work sessions maintain a maximum of two open tabs. It could be replying to mails, working on Excel sheets or PowerPoint presentations. Shut down all other tabs. If there is an interesting site, bookmark it and come back to it later. When you are having fun or researching work, by all means have lots of tabs open!

So your super simple habit is divide your working behaviours into research and deep work. During the deep work hours close all tabs. Focus on one task. This is a very simple behavioural habit to change. It has a big productivity benefit. It's one of the first changes to creating a perfect deep work environment.

Exercise

Split your tasks between research vs. deep work.

___________________	___________________
___________________	___________________
___________________	___________________
___________________	___________________
___________________	___________________
___________________	___________________
___________________	___________________

Remember to close all tabs on your browser before getting into any deep work time.

Overscheduling

Here's a fun fact: the first daily planner was introduced in 1773. Yes, more than 250 years ago! It was created by Philadelphia-based publisher Robert Aitken.

This was a planner that was divided into sections by weeks. Very similar to the way we have daily planners now. On the left-hand side pages was a place to maintain your expenses. On the right was a place for memos and meeting information.

The problem with this planner was that it was way before its time. The industrial revolution had not yet taken place, which means the administrative force had not been created. These would be the people who would really need a daily planner.

The first successful planner was launched in the 1900s and then there was an all-out fight between various companies, trying to gain traction and market share. Daily planners have mainly been used by companies as marketing or advertising collateral.

When I was a child, around the end of December and early January, we would get close to fifteen daily planners, all from different companies. My grandmother would then sit and evaluate each one. It was a very serious exercise. When she had finally decided on a diary, she would painstakingly go through each page of her previous year's diary and copy from it all the important dates like birthdays and anniversaries into the new diary. Then came all the phone numbers. One full day was dedicated to this activity. These are skill sets that have been lost now forever.

Through the year my grandmother would record on each page the amount of milk that was bought or the amount of mutton, money spent on vegetables, etc. Parties and social events were recorded in that diary. It was a log of our life for that year.

Scheduling has come such a long way since then. We don't have grannies writing notes for us and copying each birthday. The tools of scheduling have become so advanced that it is amazing how much we can do at the push of a button or the tap of a screen. Yet no one teaches us how to use it effectively.

One of the things I spend a lot of time with my clients on is scheduling their time. Most have never used a schedule in their life. Only meetings and birthdays are scheduled and then everything else is left to chance.

So when they begin scheduling, the first mistake they make is to overschedule. We are a society that believes more is better. The more we can pack into a day the better. The more I push myself the better. Well, that's not true. You see there comes a point where too much actually retards progress.

Three things happen with overscheduling, which can affect your growth.

First is that often times when we schedule too much in, we don't give ourselves enough time for relaxation or a break. We schedule one meeting after another. It is important to factor in free time, buffer time and generally time when you do nothing.

Secondly, when you overschedule you could look at the day and suddenly feel overwhelmed. OMG, I have so much to do today. This can create inertia to just start.

Finally, when you over schedule, you realise that you have only completed about 45 per cent of the things you had scheduled into your day. This makes you feel like a loser. Like you are not achieving enough. That you were unable to complete everything you had planned. The truth is that you had planned wrong. It had nothing to do with the fact that you lack discipline or are a loser.

Instead of trying harder next time, I would suggest that you reduce the number of things on your schedule. Cut down your schedule by half, if you need to. Chances are you are not ready to deal with all you have planned anyway.

Once you consistently begin completing all that you have planned, then you can go and add more to your schedule. As always, start small and grow from there. If you are not scheduling, please start.

So your super simple habit to prevent yourself from feeling like you are not achieving enough, even after planning, starts with reducing the number of things you have scheduled. You need to be realistic about the plans. Start small, and with time you'll be able to easily add more to your daily schedule.

All these high-flying CEOs with packed days and endless amounts of energy also started small and then grew from there.

Exercise

Identify the top three things to do in today's or tomorrow's schedule. These are things that only you can do and are the most urgent and important.

____

____

____

____

____

Make a list of things on your schedule that you can take off, schedule for later or outsource. Plan your work.

____

____

____

____

____

Pomodoro: The Secret Sauce

What is the first cuisine that comes to mind when you think of tomatoes? Italian, right? Pasta in that fiery arrabbiata sauce or a pizza topped with tomatoes. Tomato is in everything.

Did you know that the tomato is not native to Italy but to South America? The Spanish discovered it while they were sailing the high seas and busy colonising South America.

They brought this plant back and spread it throughout their colonies. It was then introduced to Italy and Britain. The British then spread it amongst their colonies. This is why we find it everywhere.

Tomatoes were originally smaller and orange or yellow in colour. This is how they got their name Pome D'Oro, which means golden apple. Later, they came to be called pomodoro.

The word 'pomodoro' is now linked with a productivity technique. You have heard me use the term 'deep work'. I have found deep work to be the biggest game changer for me and the work I do.

The first step towards deep work is to allocate time to focus on one task without any distractions. And using the 'pomodoro technique' makes this possible.

Francesco Cirillo developed the pomodoro technique in the late 1980s. The principle is simple. You use a timer to break down your working time into twenty-five-minute intervals. Each session of focus work is followed by a five-minute break.

It is called the pomodoro technique because the timer that Cirillo used while experimenting with the method was in the shape of a tomato. He preferred using a physical, old school method of time keeping over a fancy digital option.

There are hundreds of apps that you can use both on the computer and on your phone. Some of the phone apps will automatically put your phone on airplane mode as you are working. I either use a physical timer or my phone's timer.

The principles of the pomodoro technique are what make it powerful. There are six steps:

Decide on the task to be done.

Set the pomodoro timer to twenty-five minutes.

Work on the task.

When the timer rings, stop working and put a checkmark on a piece of paper.

If you have fewer than four checkmarks, take a short break (three to five minutes), then restart the timer. After four pomodoros, take a longer break (fifteen to thirty minutes). Reset your checkmark count to zero.

It's very simple. The trick here is that there should be twenty-five minutes of *uninterrupted work.* If the task you are doing is interrupted you cannot count that pomodoro and you have to start it all over again. Remember you can only take a long break after four completed pomodoros.

You can use one chunk of twenty-five minutes to work on one task, or you can divide up that one task over multiple twenty-five-minute pomodoros.

Different people prefer different time lengths. Some of my clients prefer a forty-minute working window. They feel it takes ten minutes to get into the zone. I prefer the twenty-five-minute method.

So this technique is asking for your full focus and attention. It's fun and challenging as well. Believe me, the challenge is restricting both internal and external distractions.

This is an excellent technique to use while working in an office or studying for an exam. Very often a task that should just take twenty minutes to do ends up taking a few hours. The cause is various distractions.

Today the primary indicator of success is how well you can focus and put your attention on one task. We live in what is now called the attention economy, where companies are doing everything that they can to pull your focus and attention. The more time you spend staring at apps on your phone, the more money these apps make. Notifications are constantly calling out to you.

Using the pomodoro technique—or other similar tools—greatly help with learning to curb these distractions. Imagine if you could finish your work in one fourth the time it usually takes?

So your super simple habit for increasing your productivity is to start using a pomodoro timer. Set a timer for twenty-five minutes and work without distractions for that time. At the end, take a five-minute break. Repeat this four times. Then take a longer thirty-minute break.

Remember, this one simple habit is the bedrock for creating pockets of time when you do deep work. Following the pomodoro technique teaches you to be distraction free.

Exercise

Keep a daily tally of how many successful Pomodoros you have completed (twenty-five minutes of work + five-minute break). Every couple of days, try increasing it.

Day one

____

____

____

____

____

____

____

____

____

____

____

____

____

____

____

____

____

Saying No Is Like Saying Yes

Do you know about contronyms? These are typically verbs or action words that have the same spelling and pronunciation but mean completely different things.

The meaning of the word changes depending on the context in which it is used. English is a funny language and things like this just make it more and more confusing.

For example, the verb, to dust. It means to remove dirt or dust. For example, I spent all day dusting the bookshelf. It can also mean to add dust or lightly powder something. Like when we say: She dusted the cake with icing sugar. Two completely different meanings.

The word 'overlook' also has a similar story. It can mean to watch carefully. Like the way your boss overlooks the work you do. It can also refer to missing out on details. He overlooked the mistake in chapter 4.

Like I said, English can be such a confusing language.

Let's talk about a problem most of us have. We find it difficult to say no to people and things. We want to say no. We decide to say no. But then when it is time to say no, you just blurt out a yes!

Why do we find it so hard to say no?

The first problem is with the word itself. We believe that no means rejection. No means not caring for the other person. No means making the other person feel like a failure. This reminds us of the times we have been rejected and how we felt about it.

The second reason we can't say no is because of the fear of missing out. FOMO is at a crazy all-time high right now. We see so many people travelling and meeting each other and we want to be a part of that. We get invited for things and have to say no, but we just can't. FOMO always makes us feel like we are being pulled in different directions.

Very often when we have an inability to say no, the quality of our own life diminishes dramatically. We get a feeling of being overwhelmed. This is because there are so many things that are happening at the same time. It becomes hard for us to focus on the things that are really important to us. This feeling is nothing but having too much on your plate and not prioritising what goes first, second and third.

Every time we say yes to things that are not important and things we don't have to do, we are technically saying no to all the things that are important to us. This is a situation we find ourselves in very often. We are forever busy doing useless things. Things of no importance.

The key thing to remember here is that every time you say no to someone, we are actually saying yes to ourself. This is so important. We have to stop living other people's lives. Every time we say yes to them, we are saying no to our lives.

As your habit coach I want you to banish this useless habit of saying yes to everyone else but yourself. You have to learn to put your needs and tasks and wants ahead of those of others.

Does that mean you should become selfish? Yes, maybe a little more selfish than you are now. Till you learn to say yes to yourself more easily.

So your super simple habit to start saying yes to yourself and the life you want begins by practising how to say no. For this week, I want you to focus on saying no to a minimum of five people. If people ask you for something, or request you to do something that you don't want to do, say no.

You aren't a bad person. They will not leave you. They will not think you are rude. Learn to say no politely without justifying why. They do not need to know why you can't do it. You can help by offering them a different solution, or point them towards someone else who can help them.

Saying no is an art and it will take practice for you to get it right. The more you work towards it the better you will be.

Exercise

What are five things that have happened recently that you wanted to say 'no' to, but ended up agreeing to?

How will you say 'no' (politely) in the same situation if it were to take place again?

Keep a track of how many 'no's' you dealt out over this week.

Slicing the Stress: The Art of Relaxing and Greater Productivity

You'd think that before the era of guns, swords were the most used weapons on the battlefield. Right? Wrong! Swords were used only by the nobility. This is because they were very expensive to produce. Most soldiers on the battlefield would have some version of a spear or pike. And this was the real weapon of war. Using spears was the most effective form of combat that needed the least amount of training.

Swords, on the other hand, were made of bronze, which was expensive. Later, steel came to be used, which was expensive too, and iron was traded all over the world to be used for making these swords.

While iron—and hence the making of the sword—was costly, what was costlier was the training needed to be able to wield the sword correctly in battle. Using a sword is not as simple as 'pointy end goes into the bad guy'. Every inch of your body is used to manoeuvre it, and attention needs to be given to every movement to make it as efficient as possible. A millisecond off could be the difference between life and death.

I remember growing up sword-fighting with my cousins. We, of course, had plastic swords. One was a He-Man sword and the other was a talwar, or the Indian curved sword. It was so much fun play-fighting, using the pillows as shields to defend ourselves. And we used to try every cool-looking move that we saw on the television.

Recently, I got interested in sword fighting again. However, this time, I wanted to learn the real techniques. So I got myself a training sword and started practising with it.

I am a fit guy but after five minutes of practice I found myself panting. My muscles were aching. If this had been a real fight, I would have been dead a long time ago.

That is when I chanced upon a video of an old Japanese teacher. He flowed effortlessly, gliding across the floor. His katana moved with such grace. You could see the years of practice that he had put into his life's work.

Throughout the video, he kept saying one thing: be relaxed.

As a new student, you hold tension in your body, in every muscle. But if you are relaxed you will be faster. If your hand grip is relaxed you can move the blade more swiftly. If your knees are relaxed you can slide left and right faster. I realised I had to relax more. And the more I relaxed, the easier the movements became.

It isn't just in a sword fight that we feel tense. Our work lives are filled with tension too. Tension literally means a pulling force, it's the exact opposite of being relaxed. And over the years of working with people, I have noticed that the more tension people are under the less productive they are.

If we are feeling stressed, overworked or agitated, we take longer to write emails and presentations. We make more mistakes, and when we have to rework the mistake, our productivity drops rapidly.

Just like on the battlefield, with our enemy in front of us, the key to success at the workplace lies in being relaxed. When we see a deadline running towards us, we must remain relaxed. Getting hyper or anxious doesn't work. We need to focus not on the deadline but on our body and our mind.

If we can maintain a state of being relaxed throughout our day, as we complete our work, we'll notice the difference in how much we are able to accomplish.

Most of us believe that work is hard, that it is stressful. When I am giving talks in corporate offices and I ask them what a day in the office looks like, everyone laughs and says it's too much stress. They do not believe that one can be relaxed and work at the same time.

So here are two habits to follow when it comes to being relaxed. I learnt these from that graceful Japanese teacher, who ended up teaching me about more than just a sword fight.

Habit one: consciously relax the muscles in the body. You can do this while sitting in the car or at your office desk. Wherever you are at that moment, consciously relax your muscles. Notice where in your body are you holding tension. Are your toes gripping your shoes? Are your fingers unconsciously tight? Are your eyes feeling strained? Are you all hunched up? Breathe in and out a few times to relax the body.

When the body is relaxed, the mind relaxes. When we relax our body, we'll notice our mind slowing down. The body and the mind are connected in this way. Have you ever noticed how people with a very active mind also have very active bodies?

Now let's get to the second habit: think about that moment and that one task only. We stay in tension because we are worrying about a presentation while typing out an email. And then when we are working on a presentation we are thinking about the email we sent.

Our mind is never on the task at hand; it is wandering all over the place. A relaxed mind is focused on one task. Multitasking is a bunch of lies; it does not exist. It takes too much energy to multitask and you end up less productive overall.

So start by focusing on the tension in your body. Relax. Then focus on the task at hand. Bring the old wisdom of a sword-fighting master. If we can get his precision and grace to the work we do, we will see our productivity levels soar.

Exercise

Notice where you hold tension in your body. Which parts of your body are tense? Fingers, eyes, forehead, neck, legs, arms? Note them down and consciously relax them.

____

____

____

____

____

Bring yourself back to the moment when your mind wanders because of stress. Write the following sentence as many times as you can in the space below, and focus on each stroke of the pen, each letter and each word. Be completely present in the moment. 'Now is all.'

____

____

____

____

____

Remember to practise these exercises every time you feel like you are tense and stressed.

The Perfect Moment

Did you know that there are three kinds of perfectionism?

The first kind of perfectionism is called socially prescribed perfectionism. This is when a person believes that others expect them to be perfect. What is interesting about this kind of perfectionism is that society or their family and friends may or may not be actually imposing it on the person, but that doesn't matter as the person takes on the pressure of perfectionism anyway. We often see this among children with very competitive or overbearing parents.

The second kind of perfectionism is self-oriented perfectionism. This is when the person imposes these unrealistic standards on themselves. They expect only the best from themselves, and if they can't deliver the best, it is unacceptable. You will be surprised at how many people suffer under the weight of their own expectations.

The third kind of perfectionism is called other-oriented perfectionism. This is when you expect others to be perfect. You transfer your unrealistic expectations to the people around you. You set very high standards for your friends and family, or even co-workers. These kinds of perfectionists are frustrating for people around and for themselves. This is because they are constantly living with expectations that cannot be met.

The interesting thing is most perfectionists are either procrastinators or frustrated with their output. I know this firsthand because my dad is a perfectionist. He is always terribly particular about the way things are done. When I used to write presentations for the company, each comma and semi-colon was agonised over.

Deciding on a holiday destination and planning the itinerary was such an agonising exercise that we never ended up travelling anywhere.

I remember trying to get a website made for our company years ago. My dad was being such a perfectionist about the website's design that we went through two designing agencies and in the end did not have a website.

Now, this is the true problem with perfectionism. Nothing ever gets done. In the quest for perfection, we just stagnate. Perfection is a fallacy. It does not exist; it can always be made better and better.

When I finished writing my first book, I felt proud of what I had achieved. So I took printouts of the manuscript and gave them to my parents to read. When I checked in after three days, Mom had finished reading seven chapters while my dad had not even started.

Dad had earlier made me feel guilty about not involving him in the writing process. I knew that he wanted to read the manuscript. When I asked him why he hadn't started yet, he told me he was waiting for the perfect moment. 'Today I will sit down with a pen and a coffee and read and make pointers and corrections to the book,' he said.

How often in life do we wait for that perfect moment to start something? How often do we sit around waiting and waiting? Hoping that inspiration will strike, or that magically everything will be just perfect.

We wait for that perfect moment to tell someone we love them, when the moonlight is just perfect and they are in a good mood. We wait for that perfect moment to ask for a raise. We wait for that perfect moment to start our new business or even post something on social media.

There is no such thing as the perfect moment. It is a lie. It does not exist. Waiting for it, only makes you a procrastinator. Not a perfectionist.

The truth is that the perfect moment is right now. The perfect moment is the moment you decide to do something and act on it. The perfect moment is this breath you are taking right now. If you truly understand this, you'll stop procrastinating and a whole world of opportunities will open up.

I believe that you have to start and then figure out what to do as things unfold. I had never written a book. But so what? I couldn't let that stop me. I thought I'd jump in and figure it out. I had never recorded a podcast. But who cares? I'd jump in and figure it out. Why live in regret of the things that could have been, if only you had tried instead of waiting for the perfect opportunity?

So your super simple habit starts by taking a deep breath and letting your idea of perfection go. Get yourself back into the moment in time that you currently inhabit. Then truly feel it and believe that that is the perfect moment. Tomorrow is a total mystery. Who knows what will happen? The only thing you truly have control over is right now.

So learn to grab the present. It is the perfect moment.

Exercise

Which kind of perfectionism do you normally display?

____

____

____

____

Perfectionism is like a death sentence to productivity. What are some things that you have not begun or completed because you are waiting for the perfect moment?

____

____

____

____

List five things you'll start on immediately instead of waiting for the perfect moment. Jump in and figure it out!

____

____

____

____

____

The Poison Called Criticism

A fun fact for you: the longest someone has spoken at a stretch is ninety hours and two minutes! I know some of you might be thinking that this record belongs to your ex-partner, but you are just being mean.

The longest speech marathon was achieved by Ananta Ram K.C. in Kathmandu, Nepal, who talked non-stop from 6.15 a.m. on 27 August to 12.17 a.m. on 31 August 2018. Now, what I find really funny is that Ananta Ram K.C. maintained a silence for almost seven days before he started with this longest speech of his.

At first, there was silence and then there was no stopping him. Ever heard about the calm before the storm?

That was about a speech, but did you know there's even a record for the longest PowerPoint presentation? The record is currently held by a group of students from Missouri who in 2017, presented for 139 hours straight! I can imagine some of you nodding your heads and saying: didn't I tell you, PowerPoint presentations are evil!

The record for the longest presentation before this was held by Ryan Allis who, in 2014, delivered one with 1,286 slides on 'Lessons from my 20's.' Can you imagine what this boy must be like now in his forties?

I love making presentations and giving talks. But never do I go over ninety minutes.

In my company, we have something called the presentation competition. Everyone gets a chance to make a presentation on a pre-decided topic. And the topic can be anything. The idea behind this is for everyone to have an opportunity to improve their presentation skills in a safe environment.

After the presentation competition is over, we usually give feedback to each participant, telling them what worked and what they can improve.

A woman who was new to the company made her first presentation at one such competition. But when we were giving feedback, she got really upset. Who do you think you are to criticise me on the presentation, she lashed out, and then went on and on about receiving 'criticism.'

Let's talk about the difference between feedback and criticism.

While growing up, most of us are exposed to a lot of criticism as we grow up. When we get criticised, we feel hurt, angry, sad, rejected, vulnerable, inadequate—the list of emotions we feel is endless.

Remember the last time that you were criticised? How did you feel? What was going through your mind? Were you in a happy place or sad?

Go back to when you were a child. Do you remember how a teacher, a parent or a friend's parent criticised you? Well, that is the same energy we bring to our daily lives as well when someone criticises us or gives us feedback.

There are many different ways to criticise and not all of them need to be hurtful. However, when we criticise we often refer to the person being good or bad. We talk about their shortcomings or their personality. It is a very personal attack and a very toxic trait.

When we give feedback, we should restrain it to what the person did. It should be about their actions, not their identity. Feedback is not supposed to hurt someone's sense of self but just show them how to do something in a different way.

When you were learning how to drive and the person teaching you said 'slow down and go smoothly over the speed breaker next time' they were giving you feedback and training you. You got better in the process.

Criticism would be if the driving instructor had told you, 'Why are you always in such a hurry, don't you know how to slow down? You can see there is a speed breaker there, can't you? Why do you want to break my suspension?'

Did you notice the difference between the two?

Feedback was constructive and about the action you took. Criticism did not tell you how to get better, it just told you what a bad person you were.

We often fall into this trap of talking to people like this. We criticise the person when it is their actions that need to change. When you label and criticise a person, it wreaks havoc with their sense of self. When we call someone selfish, bad, lazy or weak, the label sticks. They live their life like that. The more you say it, the stronger the label sticks.

Our first habit today is about receiving criticism. If someone starts criticising you, wait for them to finish, ignore what they said and ask them: Okay, so what would you like me to do next time? This way you are asking them to discuss your actions, not your identity.

The second habit is for when you give feedback. Always remember to address the person's actions, not the person's identity or personality.

We have the power to break this toxic cycle of criticism. And it always starts with us.

Exercise

Do you remember any feedback or criticism you received recently? Was it a personal attack, or was there something you could learn and put to use in your life?

____

____

____

____

Have you criticised someone recently? How would you turn that criticism into actionable feedback that they could use?

____

____

____

____

The Rule of Two: Accountability for Your Habits

To-do lists are an effective way of keeping track of things we need to do. Today, there are so many apps that allow us to make to-do lists online. But, do you know that about 83 per cent of people still prefer making handwritten lists? Yes, even in today's digital day and age.

The reason behind it is simple: nothing beats the satisfaction of striking something off your to-do list. That striking out of an item off the list—or putting a tick mark against it, if that's your style—gives one a sense of accomplishment but also, in some cases at least, a sense of relief.

Here's a fun fact: 50 per cent of the people surveyed admitted to adding already completed tasks to their to-do list. Why would they do so? Well, just so that they could tick them off the list. It's insane how much we like the idea of ticking things off.

These statistics come from a survey of over six hundred people. What is interesting is that many still had their lists from two or three years ago. The lists were like a diary of their lives.

What if a task does not get completed, you may ask. It keeps getting pushed to the next day. And then to the day after that. It is a never-ending cycle.

This is what happens to our best-intentioned habits as well.

Have you ever noticed the gusto with which you start off a new habit? Say, you decided to make meditation a part of your daily routine. Day One: You meditate. Day Two: You manage to meditate again. Day Three: You miss out on it. You feel bad and think you will make up for it the next day. Day Four: No meditation session second day in a row.

Before you know it, the week is over and you have missed five days in a row. This is what I call the rule of two.

It's perfectly normal to miss one day of a habit. We are all human and it happens to the best of us. We cannot be unnecessarily strict about it. But never ever—and I mean NEVER EVER—miss two days in a row. Because now skipping meditation or finding an excuse has become a habit.

This rule of two is very powerful, each day you miss a habit in a row, missing it becomes the behaviour. Missing your goal is now a habit.

The problem is that we then become masters of making excuses, masters of not doing what we had planned. I remember a friend of mine wanting to learn how to cycle. She missed practising three days in a row and by this third day, she had all sorts of excuses ready: I'm wearing the wrong shoes. I'm wearing the wrong skirt. I didn't eat lunch so I'm feeling woozy.

When we miss our habits, we become experts at excuses. Just like my friend did. We gain such expertise in making excuses that we believe our own made-up limitations. How many times have we heard people say: Oh, I can't give up sugar. Oh, I can't meditate. Oh, I can't wake up early. These are all just excuses we have created for ourselves.

The most devastating problem with the rule of two is that very soon we stop seeing results. And when we don't see results, we are quick to wonder: What is the point of it all? Why work so hard for something that's not even giving results?

The villain here is our short-term memory. We forget that we have been skipping the habit for the last five days. Instead we call the habit useless.

So the best way to break this rule of two is through a process called tracking. I like to use a tiny pocket book, which I carry around with me everywhere I go. Every time I have kept to my routine of any particular habit, I note it down in my pocket book. You can do it too.

Carry your own little notebook and fill it up with details. For instance,

> I meditated for twenty minutes at home.

I slept at 10.00 p.m. and woke up next day feeling refreshed.

The fact that you have to write it down gives it certain gravitas or level of importance. You are not likely to miss the habit.

The pocket book acts as a reminder. Every time you see it, you are reminded about the habits you have to reinforce that day.

The notebook also helps in breaking your bad habits.

Do you want to spend less money? Then write down every time you pay for something.

Want to quit smoking? Write down every time you light a cigarette.

Get inventive with the way you start tracking. Write down every episode you watch on Netflix to see how much time you spent on it over a week.

Tracking is a very important tool for adopting new habits.

So your simple habit to start tracking is to carry a small notepad with you and make a note of the habits you completed that day. If you absolutely refuse to carry a notepad, get a habit tracking app from the app store.

Have a weekly review of how the habits are shaping up. And remember, never ever miss two days in a row—that's the golden rule of building new habits. As I have mentioned in my first book: *Change Your Habits Change Your Life*.

Exercise

Get a small notepad that fits in your pocket. Carry it around with you every day and just start noting down all the daily habits you are trying to change.

____

____

____

____

Write down three habits that you want to start tracking. Put a tick mark or a tally mark next to the habit you complete each day.

____

____

____

____

The Slot Machine in Our Pocket: Mobile Addiction and a Rehab Plan

Have you ever tried your luck at a slot machine where the best outcome is to get three symbols of the same kind in a row?

Here's a fun fact: the slot machines in casinos are designed to be extremely addictive. They are designed to make you feel like you are almost winning. Each time the machine rolls, you hold your breath in anticipation. One symbol is revealed at a time, and with each symbol showing up, one gets a hit of dopamine. The feeling of almost winning makes you want to play again and again and again.

Slot machines are super simple. They don't make our brains work hard. And that's by design. There is instant gratification and the brain lights up as if it were on drugs. Gambling becomes an addiction. People refer to slot machines as the cocaine of gambling. The scary truth is that we carry a slot machine around with us every day. We have it in our pockets. I am referring to our mobile phones.

Our phones and social media apps have been designed to be addictive—often by the same people who design slot machines.

Think about it. We are always anticipating a message. The notifications on the phone are a constant slow drip of dopamine. Notifications communicate a desire that someone wants you. That is very similar to the feeling of almost winning.

Look at how we scroll through our social media. It's easy to do and completely brainless. We have to keep checking the phone to see if someone has liked our picture or post. Mobile phones are slot machines in our pockets.

More than half the listeners of my podcast *The Habit Coach* have reached out to me with a request to help them get out of their phone addiction. *I can't put my phone away. If it is not next to me, I get anxiety.* I often receive these kinds of messages. Many of my coaching clients too are addicted to their phones.

The top three reasons for the phone addiction being so bad are:

1. It plays with our sense of self-worth. If people are not liking our photograph, or if no one has messaged us for a while, we start questioning ourselves. Looking at all the pictures of people having fun and looking beautiful gives us an inferiority complex. What we don't realise is that the bad pictures never make it to social media. Everyone always shows their life the way they wish it was. Since our self-worth is getting determined by the comparisons we draw between our actual lives and only the good parts of other people's lives, the odds are heavily stacked against us.

2. It affects our productivity. Do we even realise that when we have our phone next to us while working, every time it beeps or vibrates—whether it is for a call, a message or just a notification for someone having posted something on Instagram or Twitter (now X)—it distracts us. While we think we are multitasking, we are indulging in what is known as task switching. Science has proven that we can't multitask. We can only rapidly switch between tasks. This means there is no way we can remain productive while checking our phone constantly. In this era of distractions, the art of deep work is lost to us.
3. We start developing social anxiety. We have got so used to speaking to people via chat that a phone call is now too weird. What's worse is that the new generation born into this era of mobile phones often shows signs of not being able to interact face to face. They lack the skills to read body language and to make conversation.

How do we ensure that our mobile phones act as a useful tool rather than becoming the bane of our lives? It's simple. All we need to do is follow some rules for phone usage:

Step 1: Switch off all notifications. Your phone should not beep or vibrate or turn on for anything but a phone call. This means all email, social media, chats and apps can't access you, unless you want to access them.

Step 2: Identify two or three hours when you'll keep your phone switched off or put it away in a drawer. Do this every single day. Use this time to focus on anything that you have not been able to focus on. Do deep work, that is, tasks that need concentration. If you still find yourself checking your phone during these hours, hand your phone to a friend or colleague with strict instructions to return it to you only once your time is up.

Step 3: Once a week leave your phone at home and go for a walk. When you start doing it, it will be the weirdest feeling ever. But I can guarantee you that you'll soon realise that you don't need your phone every single minute of the day. The world is not full of emergencies that will need your constant attention.

No notifications, three hours of focused work a day and a phone-free walk every week—this super simple yet effective rehab plan can help you claim your life back.

Remember that phones and apps are designed by companies to be addictive. For them, that's the route to profits. It is up to us to ensure our well-being by not getting dragged into this addiction.

Exercise

Get rid of that needy phone by switching off all the notifications from various apps. You can do this under your phone settings.

Did you do it? ____

Fix a time of the day that you will spend without your phone. Can you do without your phone one hour at a go?

____

____

____

____

Decide on one day when you will go on a phone-free walk. Fix a time for this so you can form a habit. Gradually, you may want to make it a daily habit.

____

____

____

____

University on Wheels

Those of us living in cities like Delhi, Mumbai and Bengaluru, have resigned to our fate when it comes to long commutes and traffic jams. According to a study conducted by researchers, the ideal time to work should be sixteen minutes. Any less and we don't feel like leaving home for work, or we misjudge the time and run late.

The truth of our lives is several minutes away from that figure though. On an average, people around the world spend forty minutes travelling to work and another forty minutes back home. Most of us in Mumbai spend more than an hour each way. All these hours begin to add up. By the end of the month you have spent more than a full day just travelling to and from work.

I was fascinated by a study conducted in Sweden, where they defined long commute as one that's longer than forty-five minutes. They discovered that couples that have to deal with long commutes tend to have higher divorce rates. According to another study, couples who travel to work in the same direction tend to be more satisfied with their relationship.

Weird marital facts aside, the commute to work is a big hit on our individual lives and productivity. Long commutes to and from work decrease our chances of exercising or cooking a meal at home. They impact the amount of time we get to spend bonding with our families. Long commutes can even reduce our sleeping hours as we try to catch up with our home lives and responsibilities by keeping awake longer.

The commute to work, however, is a necessary evil. Not everyone can choose to work remotely. Given that we can't often do anything about our long commutes, our goal should be to make the best of what we've got. We can turn these wasted hours into something productive.

I often have to travel close to three hours in a day shuttling between client meetings. I use this time to expand my knowledge. On these commutes I listen to podcasts or audiobooks. I call this time my university on wheels.

I don't complain. I don't waste my time listening to music. I go about grappling with interesting ideas and thought processes on my university on wheels. I learn new skills.

There is a saying that I really love: 'A mind once expanded by a larger idea never returns to its original size.'

My love for podcasts started with this simple idea, and it eventually led me to create *The Habit Coach* podcast for you. Each fun fact or habit that I talk about in my podcast is something that can open our minds to new possibilities.

The first podcast series I listened to was called *A History of the World in 100 Objects*. This was over five years ago. Then I started listening to *Optimize* by Brian Johnson and *The Model Health Show*. And there was no turning back after that.

Audiobooks are another fantastic way to gain new knowledge and information. They are convenient for long commutes and are as affordable as a normal paperback edition. And some of the narrators are such good storytellers, which only adds to the experience. You can even listen to my first book as an audiobook on Audible.

So the super simple habit for you to adopt is to download a podcast or an audiobook app. Search for shows you might enjoy listening to or a book that might interest you.

Remember, you can exercise your mind by learning new things. And in the digital age that we live, it's so easy to tune into your own university on wheels.

Exercise

Make a list of topics you are currently interested in. A hobby or a business skill you are trying to acquire.

____

____

____

____

Identify a timeslot when you can listen to a podcast or an audiobook regularly. This will help you form a habit of it.

____

____

____

____

Come back and write down five things that you've learnt on your University on Wheels.

____

____

____

____

Upskill to Upgrade Your Mind

Did you know that over the next five years, there will be a churn of 23 per cent in the workforce of the world? This means that 12.3 per cent of the jobs will become irrelevant because of technology and 10.2 per cent of new jobs will become relevant because of that same technology.

This comes from a report presented at the World Economic Forum, Davos. This is the biggest forum in the world, where all the world leaders come to discuss the state of global economics and the impact it will have across business and people.

Now I am fed up with most people looking at technological change as a bad thing. They are thinking too small and they are thinking like victims.

What they don't realise is that technology always leads to an increase in jobs in the long run. History is a testament to this. In the short term, of course, technology is a disruptor. Its role, after all, is to change things for the better. If you don't want to change, that is when all the problems start.

Instead of just focusing on job churn or job loss as a statistic, change your perspective. There is a more empowering statistic to look at. The same report mentions that over the next five years job skills will change by 44 per cent. That means that 44 per cent of the workforce will need to learn new skills.

This is the most important statistic of all.

I have been saying this on my podcast *The Habit Coach*, for over five years now—we need to learn and upskill constantly. Now, it has become the most important thing to do.

What does upskilling mean? It means you are learning a new way of working, but more importantly, you are learning a new way of thinking. When you learn a new skill, you are forced to look at the world around you differently. For example, if you learn how to look at database analytics for the first time, you will start seeing databases all around you.

If copywriting is your newly acquired skill, then, you will start seeing well-written emails and advertisements around you. Upskilling changes the way you think.

The Davos report also identifies three skills as the most important: cognitive problem-solving; analytical thinking and technology literacy.

Apart from this, there are some skills that I feel are golden and will always be important for us, irrespective of what happens to the world. The first skill is learning how to sell. Selling your ideas to someone. Selling your suggestions to your boss. Or selling the movie you want to watch to your partner. We all need to learn how to sell.

The second is storytelling. Learning how to tell stories is very important as it helps you convey your message in the most impactful way. Humans have always told stories and hence we have a strong desire to learn and communicate using storytelling.

The third skill is negotiation. This is important because it will help you get a new job and salary hikes. It will help you seek new opportunities and then help you get them. Negotiation is not bargaining for clothes at the roadside shop on fashion street. Negotiation is about finding win-win situations.

Apart from this, play around with different AI tools or with tools like Canva. Dive into technology without being hesitant. Make mistakes while learning because that is the way you will learn a new skill.

A good rule of thumb is to learn three new skills every six months. You can learn one new skill at a time, or you can learn all three at the same time. Just put thirty minutes aside every day.

These three new skills will help skyrocket your career and your life. Keep learning and changing with the environment around you.

This super simple habit starts by asking yourself, have you learnt anything new or done anything new for your job in the last six months. If not, start today. Just take out thirty minutes every day and learn a new skill. You can do this by reading up or by enrolling for an online course. It's super simple, just try it. And I promise, the benefits will be there for you to see.

Exercise

What are three new skills that you need to learn to have the biggest growth in your career or life?

1. ____

2. ____

3. ____

How do you plan to learn these skills? Online courses? Mentors? Youtube? Books?

____

____

____

____

How can you use AI to help you acquire or develop new skills?

____

____

____

____

Acknowledgements

I would like to thank the amazing people at Westland for publishing this book. The hard work and dedication needed to bring out a book is truly exceptional and without the team at Westland none of this would've been possible.

I would also like to thank IVM and Pratilipi for supporting me and partnering with me for *The Habit Coach* podcast and making it the incredible success that it is.

Scan this code and download the
'100 Day Productivity Planner'

Scan this code for the explainer video
for the '100 Day Productivity Planner'